Buoyancy

a memoir

Praise for *Buoyancy*

Jeannie begets love and that love grows from her and beyond her and then grows some more. Her family, friends, community, art, poems, gardens, beloved dogs, fun-loving smart-ass sense of humor, candor, vulnerability, and indomitableness are revealed in these pages.

—*Amy Ballestad,*
Poet, Artist, Teacher, Administrator Heart of the Beast Puppet and Mask Theatre; Founding Member Powderhorn Writers Festival

So much love is in this memoir! Only a fine poet whose touch is light as a feather can levitate her readers with words the way Jeannie Piekos does with her cancer memoir, *Buoyancy*. This book and its author are beautiful and brave and strong and will make readers feel beautiful and brave and strong.

—*Mike Hazard,*
Writer whose companion is a cancer survivor

As a poet, Jeannie Piekos has demonstrated a gift for the image that pulls the reader out of habitual and trivial ways of seeing, and into depth. As a person, she has weathered a harrowing journey into life-threatening illness without letting her soul be intimidated. She knows that the question is not whether our hearts will break, but rather "what we do with their brokenness." With *Buoyancy*, she has done a fine thing.

—*Thomas R. Smith,*
Author of The Foot of the Rainbow *and* The Glory

Cancer is a scourge upon the modern human landscape. In this deeply personal memoir, Jeannie Piekos reflects with poetic beauty on the harsh realities of cancer treatment and the saving grace of human connection. Through her honesty and strength, she invites us into the fullness of life, no matter what the day may bring.

—*Rev. Mary Bohman,*
Hospice Chaplain, Cancer Survivor

This memoir grapples with the uncertain journey of cancer and the discovery of how it changes everything in life. Through poems and vignettes of a soul swept into the swirling waters of this murky disease, Jeannie Piekos' *Buoyancy* delivers an honest mixture of the dark rages and fears following diagnosis as well as the balm necessary to rediscover one's inner core. All of us should hope to handle the disease's ambiguities and diminishments with the same grace and ingenuity Jeannie Piekos presents in this book.

—*Lynette Reini-Grandell,*
Author of Approaching the Gate *and* Wild Verge

I just got a deep drink from the Jeannie Piekos' memoir, *Buoyancy*! Cancer is experienced as metaphor and as distressed flesh. Cancer is despair, a daily companion, and a relentless teacher full of the surprises of the unknown. At times, in retrospect, the cancer journal and journey can eventually be seen as a painful blessing. Jeannie's writing, both the poetry and narrative, is an engaging read. It is practical and mystical. It also possesses what proves to be a saving grace: The struggle of the writer to write with no escape from being the engaged patient. Cancer happens to the individual and all who love the person so challenged to battle on three fronts: The disease itself, the blessings and curse of the medical system, and in the field of the writer who translates the lived experience into words for the world to read. Thank the Goddess, this woman bounced back up to the surface!

—*Louis Alemayehu,*
Educator, Environmental Justice Organizer, Oral Poet, Spiritual Elder

Buoyancy

a memoir

Buoyancy: a memoir

ISBN: 978-1-7321539-0-5
eISBN: 978-1-7321539-1-2

Printed in the United States of America by Bookmobile
First edition

Cover photo: Will Hommeyer
Design & production: Sue Filbin

For information about *Buoyancy*—the memoir and the movie—or for readings and showings, please contact Jeannie at jeanniepiekos@gmail.com

Dedication

To my family, both of blood and spirit,
who are always near to my heart,
regardless of distance, form, or temporality.

Table of Contents

I am floating above them

A shore of stars sparkling in the sand

Foreword

Sickness offers a frightful gift—the opportunity to deepen a friendship from the taken-for-granted days of health into and through the every-day-counts days of illness. Jeannie's illness, or more precisely, Jeannie's approach to illness, transformed our three decades of casual-but-fond friendship into an intimate bond.

Jeannie in health: Mom, mate, poet, erotic personage, arts activist, yogi, cook, volunteer, joker, glamourpuss, dog lover, entrepreneur, seeker, hiker, camper, reader, crafter, griever, sister, grandma.

Jeannie in sickness: All of the above. Add: Warrior, sufferer, patient, frightened, determined human. Before the cancer, Jeannie embodied health and cultivation of health. After the diagnosis, she forged a kind of healthy illness. Negotiating the medical maze, enduring the poisons, loving her helpers, hating the restrictions, accepting the restrictions, facing the void, hoping, meditating, downward dogging, making poems. She was frighteningly thin, beautifully bald.

If you first meet Jeannie in these pages, you'll discover a poetic voice that speaks of anguish and hope, loneliness and love. Through the poems, essays, and CaringBridge excerpts, you'll meet a vulnerable, confused, determined, and reflective person. If you already know her, you'll know her better, deeper.

Jeannie's decision to document her cancer journey in a real-time film made by friend Will Hommeyer might have become risky over-exposure, an extra burden during the time of treatment. (Ask her stalwart husband Randy.) But the film and this memoir express the essential Jeannie, a poet whose inner life demands to be shared through the public rituals of writing and film.

Her cancer was one of many challenges she greeted with poetry. Every winter, as the days shrink to suffocating darkness and winter chills our bones, Jeannie writes a solstice poem made into a card companioned with lovely collages reminding us that winter brings its own kind of beauty. In 2005 she sent us "Deepest Night."

Since it is better for my soul
To love the thing I want to fight
I throw my heart across miles of snow.

The year before she reminded herself and us why she writes. The 2004 poem describes the frustrations of the writer (type, erase, sit, think/moan, delete, underline, cut, paste, curse). But pain begat gain for this generous poet and her chosen audience:

Here is my poem, my gift
And now you have just given
your gift to me.
It was perfect—just what I wanted,
Thank you.

Jeannie turned to poetry to help say goodbye to her dearest friend. Taking a final sad trip to California, she wanted certain poems to read to Janice in her last days. I remember Jeannie's usual languid long-legged stride diminished to a melancholy trudge up my back walk to borrow a book of poems by Linda Hogan.

When poet Roy McBride, our mutual old friend, lay dying, hooked up to a maze of alienating machinery, unable to talk, I was completely confused about how to greet or comfort him. As I tried to hold his flailing hand, Jeannie grabbed a book of poems by Lyle Daggett that lay on the table, flipped it open, and began reading in a loud determined voice intended to penetrate the illness muddling Roy's consciousness. Her voice overrode the incessant buzz and whirl of monitors and tubes. Roy quieted, smiled, and shut his eyes.

In "Integrity," the first poem in her 2005 chapbook *Held Up To The Light,* Jeannie anticipated (in some great unconscious psychic swirl) the force that would overtake her nine years later.

… no matter how they shook and twisted
the kaleidoscope
my life was still always right there.
Held up to the light, it was beautiful and endlessly
unfolding,
one miracle after another.

Whether by grace or modern medicine or force of will or the alchemy of those powers, Jeannie lives on in the light to tell her story.

Thanks, Dear.

—Flo Golod, a retired nonprofit professional, lives, writes, and gardens in Minneapolis

Preface

Cancer threw me into a vortex, agitated and spun me around until I was completely disoriented—and then spit me back out into vaguely familiar, but eerily not-quite-right territory. In writing and assembling this memoir, I felt the absurdity of trying to make sense of the messiness of disease, of trying to cram the entirety of my experience into a tidy, outlined format, to impose expository control on the discombobulation of cancer and create order out of the bedlam of disease. It's near impossible.

I can recall in vivid detail intense individual instances like sitting in the chemo chair, my head stuffed with the cotton of liquid Benadryl flowing through my port while trying to hold onto a thin thread of conversation with the friend sitting beside me, all the time hearing the buzz of other cancer patients and staff around me like a swarm of wasps batting against the window of my consciousness. But it's much more difficult to pull the lens further back in order to get the wide-angle shot that catches the whole panorama of disease.

My relationship with time transformed with disease. In fact, I am still in some ways spiraling around and around the past three years, trying to make sense of all that happened. I see myself so strong and healthy then suddenly diminished, heartsick, crying. I see myself alternately devastated, optimistic, brave, resigned, and hopeful. I see the missed opportunities and the blessings I would never name as such. I keep coming back around and around on that spiral, wondering who I am now and what I have learned—if I have learned anything.

My story fluctuates and mutates depending on the anecdotes and experiences I choose to relate. Drastically different versions emerge, and each one is true in its own right. I ask myself, *Which story do I need to tell?* The one in which I am heroically fighting cancer with barbed wit and bald head? Or the one in which I stoically endure by putting one foot in front of the other day after sickening day?

The tidy memoir of my imagination was never written. Instead, I created a mosaic from the tesserae, the catastrophic, and mundane moments of living with my diagnosis. A cancer mosaic made from sharp shards of glass, angles of metallic splinters and porcelain, cracked and broken by time. The pattern is interspersed with smooth, heart-shaped pebbles and cowrie shells, shimmering pink and translucent. I run my fingers along the surface and find the pieces are safer now to touch.

Before you are the pieces of my cobbled-together path, a conglomeration of writing from scribbled journal entries and CaringBridge posts to poetry that arose from my lamentations, as well as the reflections I wrote after the completion of treatment. Sometimes familiar, trusted words failed to communicate the devastation and complexity of disease. I trust that this composite—this mosaic with all its inherent shadow and light—will illustrate the story I need to tell.

A writer friend of mine read an early draft of this memoir and he decried (as if he had to defend me from myself), "But Jeannie, you are so much more than cancer." Of course, that's true. I am so much more than cancer. But somehow, upon diagnosis, cancer has a way of dominating the story, changing the plot, superimposing itself over the protagonist. Sometime after surgery, the port installation, and a round or two of chemo, disease became a part of my identity. Just as apparent as the radiation tattoos on my body, cancer was engraved upon my identity. Not that I am only sick. And not that illness was somehow inherently in my nature. Hardly. But disease is what I came head-to-head with; it has been my biggest challenge. And so, in my curriculum vitae, I include: *Person experiencing cancer.* I hope someday I might spiral around again and see I have evolved into: *Person surviving cancer* or who knows?—*Person often forgetting she has cancer.*

I have set sail on a boat of promises

"Feel the waves of tenderness,
the buoyancy."
—Rumi

Introduction

In the five years before my diagnosis, I was a witness to much disease and death. It seemed as if a swift and deadly scythe of cancer came through and cut a swath through my community, taking with it beloved friends and family members.

The swath began with breast cancer in my dearest friend, Janice, in 2009. When first diagnosed she was confident she could beat it. For a few years she flourished with her natural and holistic approach. But three years later the cancer metastasized. It was everywhere. When I held her hand it was limp. Her body was desiccated. Hospice was called. Janice died in September of 2012. Her death split my heart in two. From that moment on, I would live in a world without her.

In 2010, my older brother, Larry, one of twins, was diagnosed with colorectal cancer, stage three. Throughout 2011 he dealt with a brutal surgery and exhausting chemo and radiation treatment. For six years until his death, Larry suffered the debilitating aftershocks of his cancer and his cancer treatment.

Cancer and disease continued to ricochet around me. I would barely receive news that someone was sick before hearing they had stage-three or stage-four cancer. I mourned the death of another dear friend, gone before his daughter graduated high school, read the heartbreaking CaringBridge posts from friends whose husbands entered the hospital with vague symptoms only to find they had stage-four cancer, and tried to make sense of another friend's complicated, incurable disease.

At the end of 2013 the echo of cancer continued to reverberate around us. We learned that John, my husband's brother, was diagnosed with glioblastoma, a brain cancer that when diagnosed, is always stage four. The news came after weeks of mysterious injuries and bodily calamities. There was no cure. He died less than a year later when I was in the midst of treatment.

Witnessing the disease of others did nothing to prepare me for, or even make me suspect, a cancer of my own. The late, often-catastrophic diagnoses of my family and friends were alarming, but I lived in the blissful bubble of naiveté regarding my own mortality. I took good care of myself—eating the rainbow, weight-training, yoga, daily walks, moderate alcohol, lots of love. All that good care bestowed on me an infallibility. If I had a concern for my own mortality, I shelved it—archived it far from sight. What I had seen in others' diagnoses, but concealed from my conscious self, was that cancer was often lurking just out of view; it was looming and blooming in the dark mystery of the body. It was secretive, swift, and deadly.

Try entering "cancer memoir" into your search engine. The staggering numbers of pages that will appear are overwhelming. Before my diagnosis I had never read any of these memoirs. Now I've read several and there are many others still on my reading list. I imagine there will be more I will add to my list that have yet to be published. There will always be more.

From these other cancer memoirs I see that there isn't one correct way through cancer. Each cancer is unique—how it insinuates itself into a person's life, the toll it takes, the options one can choose to fight it, humble it, or try to wrestle it into remission.

But common to all these stories is the sense of loss—the sense that, if you are lucky enough to survive the cancer and the treatment, there is no going back to the person who was once healthy, vital, and oblivious to mortality. Loss is the haunting, ubiquitous theme.

I am still learning to live with mine.

A Vow to My Higher Truth

When I began working on this memoir, I read through an old journal kept long before my diagnosis. In it was a children's book idea—written with my new granddaughter in mind—some poems, a bittersweet memorial piece I had written for a friend who had passed, and dreams written in pencil, faded and feathery, caught on paper first thing in the morning.

One dream came back to me vividly. I was at a commencement ceremony of some sort. I said to another woman, "You basically have a contract with everyone you meet. You have a contract with your spouse although they might leave you or let you down. You have a contract with your children even though they grow up and away. The only person in your life who will always be with you is you. Why don't you have a contract with yourself?"

I remember thinking upon waking: *What was that about? What would a contract with myself look like? Why would I need one?*

In the two weeks after I received my doctor's bleak call, I was completely overwhelmed. The lights had suddenly gone out in my life and I felt crushed by the stampede of my own emotions. My amygdala was screaming at me, *Monsters. Run!* But there was nowhere I could escape. All that adrenaline was exhausting. I couldn't properly breathe in that panicked state. The doctors hurried me through the medical processes at an alarming speed but my brain's processor moved in slow motion.

The days went by in a blur of unfamiliar procedures that later would become routine—CT scans, oncology appointments, and blood work. There was also the emotional strain of telling friends and family, and negotiating hours of phone calls, visits, emails, and tears. I was fortunate to have incredible support from my family and friends. They advocated for me, cooked for me, and loved me.

But the emotional work of gauging my level of despondency, of keeping dread at bay, and calming the animal panic was mine alone. That emotional work was paramount. I felt like I might drown in the sudden tsunami that was my life. I needed to find a way that I could better ride out the tumultuous wave.

Writing has always been essential to me—it was especially so during my cancer treatment. The act of writing slowed down the forces around me, helped me catch my breath. But it didn't come easy. I had a hard time just forming words into sentences. It seemed I had lost the ability to communicate or that I was writing in a foreign language.

The morning after I received my diagnosis, alone in my living room and squinting in the bright May sunshine, I opened a new journal and made my first entry. It was a raw, succinct paragraph. Hardly literary, but pained and pitiful. Three days later I stumbled through a description of the Sisyphean daily task of finding calm. It began to get easier as I wrote more—recording the bizarre mechanics of creating my own CaringBridge page while being haunted by the memory of friends whose lights had gone out on that website. Or recounting the recurring dream that had me endlessly, exhaustively walking through labyrinths in search of some unknown, treasured thing.

Surprisingly, it was CaringBridge that most provided a conduit to myself. My posts, initially obligatory and quotidian, made me responsible to an audience, to keep them informed about the minutiae of my health; how my sutures were healing, what my neutrophil levels were, and what neutrophils even were.

But soon my posts were about more than the mundane details of a failing body. Writing was an arena in which I could grapple with cancer spiritually and emotionally. I was writing into a great unknowingness, writing as a process of discovery. I wanted to rise above the pitfalls of what my body was undergoing. Intimations of mantras or affirmations appeared in my posts. My own words glimmered back to me from my journal and computer screen and created pinpricks of starlight that incrementally lit up the inky darkness around me. If I could write into this potentiality of contentment, into the possibility of being fully alive right at that very moment, maybe, I could achieve it.

Time and again, through the evolution of writing, I arrived at an oasis of attentive acceptance. Sparingly and fleetingly, it glowed and illuminated the path around me. However, I found that staying there was tenuous at best. That the sanctuary I had discovered could shimmer and disappear—like a mirage. And though my landing was precarious, fizzling and fading underneath my feet, the only way forward was to just begin again—to spiral around and write once more about the path I was traveling. Immersed in the torrent of cancer treatment there was never a shortage of material.

I drafted my posts as I fell into the quagmire of cancer, scribbling notes on prescription receipts and discharge papers. Through the constant dance of poisoning and partially healing, through the renegotiation with my body of what I could no longer do and the bartering with spirit to stay in the game, I kept returning to the page. In every post, my words in black on a white page were proof to me that I was still here. As my life was coming apart, writing was the thread I needed to sew it back together.

It was a bedraggled garment I was attempting to patch. And hardest of all were the intricate stitches of poetry. I was too clumsy. The ugly task of taking my horrible reality and putting it into stanzas made me feel inadequate. My feelings were cumbersome. My emotions ineffable, complex, and hard to pare down. But I was a poet, wasn't I? I feared that poetry, like my body, was failing me, too.

But as I continued to write in my journal, and on CaringBridge, I saw something was emerging. I had been invoking the same metaphoric image over and over. I felt a shift. The image carried me to the edge of discovery. The poem that was taking shape would ferry me across. The metaphor is everywhere in my posts, journal entries, and in this very essay, in words like tsunami, waves, and drowning. Five weeks after diagnosis I wrote my poem, *Buoyant*—a lifeline I could grasp.

From the moment I received my diagnosis I was struggling against a brutal storm in the middle of a bottomless ocean. The skies around me turned a dangerous purple. The rain pelted my face in torrents. I was alone and there were fins in the distance. In the violence of the water I was sinking under the weight of despair and apprehension. Briny creatures lurked in the fathomless depth below me. In all the uncertainty, one thing I was sure of was that if I stayed in this state of shock and panic I would sink to the murky black bottom.

My rational, logical mind was beset with statistics, timeframes, and incomprehensible poisons. But the poet place in me—that mysterious channel that sometimes opens to reveal a glimpse of the infinite—tossed me a tether. *Buoyant* was the treasured thing—what I had been searching for in sporadic, chemo-fueled dreams and in the rigors of my writing. It is an uncomplicated poem with a simple directive that told me that in order to stay afloat, I had to trust that the water wasn't completely hostile. Staying buoyant meant I could not constantly fight the surge. I could not stop the rain. I had one imperative and that was to keep my head above water.

Buoyant was this poet's prayer—a meditative response to the primal fear deep within the ancestral parts of my body. Oftentimes, I was in over my head. I was afraid I might drown. But, maybe, instead of flailing, I could float. It was a simple message but not a simple mission. Like prayer and writing, it was a constant practice, but once the poem was conceived, the possibility of buoyancy remained within me.

Buoyant

> *"Feel the motions of tenderness around you, the buoyancy."*
> *—Rumi*

I have set sail on a boat of promises.

It appears it might be leaking.

The night is dark. My way unmapped.

Here in this ocean of dreams
there be monsters.
Unseen in the deep, dark below
they are briny and clawed.

I am floating above them
in my vessel of transformation.
The wind is with me. My sail is set.

I am heading toward a shore of stars
sparkling in the sand.

In the yoga nidra I practiced during cancer treatment, I was introduced to the concept of sankalpa. A sankalpa is a profound personal resolve spoken in present tense as if it is a current reality. In Sanskrit *san* means connection to the highest truth and *kalpa* means vow. A vow to my highest truth. Or, as I came to view it, a contract with oneself.

Throughout treatment (and beyond) *Buoyant* reminded me that struggling *against* only exhausted me; that *accepting* gave me the space and contentment to find joy where I was—that my life was not on pause because of illness.

Buoyant fixed an image in my mind. I was in my vessel. I had my vow. Keep my head above water. Lose the baggage that weighed me down. Feel the motions of tenderness around me.

In my vessel of transformation I could float above.

Belize

On the last day of 2013 my husband Randy and I celebrated our twenty-fifth wedding anniversary. It felt epic and extraordinary. I wanted to go on a celebratory trip that honored the years of endurance, compromise, and love. I planned our adventure for months. I emailed guides, lodges, and eco-resorts. I read everything I could. I picked Belize because they had a variety of environments. It was tropical but not overly touristy. It was a world heritage site, there was a range of cultures, it was affordable, and the official language was English.

We left on February 3, 2014. In my travel journal I noted every gorgeous sunset and each howler monkey scrambling through the treetops. I recorded the wonders of a mojito made with freshly ground sugarcane and muddled mint. I wrote about the jungle hike that took us to the top of a mountain where we were the only people. And how we stood in the mist that overlooked the clouds while our heads spun with humidity, our own sweat, and the beauty of the forest below. I mused about the tranquil blue ocean, the beautiful smiles on the Garifuna drummers, and the sublime pleasure of tea, steaming and delicious, delivered first thing in the morning on a tray.

I never wrote about the postmenopausal bleeding I was experiencing. I never mentioned the spotting or if I had any curiosity or concern about the fact that it was happening throughout this month-long anniversary trip.

Home

While Randy and I were away on our adventure in Belize, mostly without cellphone service or Internet connections, we received no bad news. No reports of loved ones who had gotten sick. No bad prognoses or stagings of cancer. But inside me something was quietly ticking. After we returned home I contemplated the postmenopausal bleeding I was experiencing. Without urgency I called my clinic. It took a couple of weeks before I could get an appointment. Finally, I saw my doctor. More appointments ensued. First for an ultrasound. Then a biopsy. On the first Friday of May at 5:30 p.m. I had a cancer diagnosis of my own—uterine papillary serous carcinoma, stage three, an aggressive, rare endometrial cancer.

The Truth of the Matter is We Really Are Alone

This is not said in anger or desperation. It is not said to gain reassurance. It is in no way a reflection on my family and friends. But still it is truth. I am here alone in my heart, my head, my body with this diagnosis of cancer. And although it will affect other people I am the one going through it; through the wondering, the waiting, the probing, and the pictures; through the cutting and the chemicals alone. It is my body; my one constant companion for fifty-seven years that will survive it or not.

I know there is a door, and I know I might go through it, too. Alone.

—journal entry one day after diagnosis

Last Night

Randy and I attempted to go out on an ordinary date—like we weren't broken and miserable. We went to our neighborhood bistro, ordered wine, flatbread pizza, and cried at the table. The waitress slipped me her reiki therapy card with the check.

Once home, I decided we had to try to make love. It felt imperative to have a final hurrah before who knows what would happen to my innermost workings. That was a lot of pressure. I didn't know if I could handle having sex. I was afraid of the emotion; afraid of us not working.

So we lay naked, side by side, and quiet, each in our own thoughts. Gradually we turned to one another. I tried to empty my mind into the sensation of touch; to experience touch without any expectation of result. I let go of thoughts. I let my body do what it knows how to do.

I had a sense of pure calm and then the moment of beautiful release ... which transformed instantaneously into a howl and tears, tears, tears. I had felt it building inside me. First desire, and then anguish rising, cascading out in a surge of emotion, relief, and surrender. Throughout our rhythm of sex, I felt my uterus inside me, thrumming.

I cried for a moment, overwhelmed yet oddly hopeful at what we had experienced. In the darkness, before sleep, Randy told me when he first heard about the diagnosis he felt that if he totally let himself go with the grief it would be unbearable for both of us.

And then, we fell off to sleep, still side by side, but closer; still weary, and with the same challenges before us, yet restored in our ability to face them.

This was an act we have consummated countless times. And yet, even after all these years, I can't take it for granted. It took a leap of faith to trust our bodies' wisdom, to believe in their resilience, and in the greater connection they could provide.

—*journal entry one week after diagnosis*

Building It

The mornings are the hardest. I am disoriented from a dream of walking my dog in the rain. In the dream there are huge puddles. I don't know which way to go. Some kids are playing catch nearby. A child misses and the ball rolls to my feet.

Then I awake to an unfamiliar and heavy weight. My body aches. My emotions swell. I feel the guilt of abandoning my children and the pain I'll cause my husband. Every maudlin thought from the trite, *Why me? Why now?* to the miserable sadness of grandchildren growing up not knowing me, of my husband remarrying, of my kids without the rudder of mom goes through my head. The things I wished to do, the woman I hoped to become, pour in through the gaping wound of emotional exhaustion. I spin out of control for maybe ten minutes before I cannot stand it any longer.

I get out of bed and do the little things that add up to a daily life. I take care of Sadie who is a practical dog. Cancer or not she needs to pee, to eat, to get a biscuit because she's a good girl. All of this I do regardless of the weight that grinds away at me. I make tea and, surprisingly, there is still happiness in the cup. I eat oatmeal.

I try to find the calm and strength that had stabilized me the night before. But it has disappeared. I realize it is something I have to create anew every day, piece by piece. It is something of my own making, my own design. It's not inherent or innate in me. I have to choose it, define it, and design it again and again. This realization is daunting but it is my task now. Build the calm.

And then somewhere in the night it is knocked down again. So I start each morning with the weight, the dog, the tea, and my task before me.

—journal entry three days after diagnosis

Surgery

It is the morning of surgery. These ten days have been a whirlwind. I'm pretty tired. The Ambien helped with sleep but I had to take quite a bit and still was awake for a while in the middle of the night and then awake early today. Not eating at all today. I wonder what I will weigh tomorrow. This is not a preferred weight-loss plan.

Yesterday was Mother's Day. Celebrating motherhood the day before my hysterectomy felt just too ironic for words. But it helped to normalize things to have good food and for the family to be together. My son, Nate, made perfect Eggs Benedict, which is my specialty, of course. He found his own recipe for the hollandaise and it was fabulous. He made it differently than I normally do. Let's see if I can remember what he said. And isn't this an unusual space for a recipe?

Nate's Hollandaise Sauce
1/4 cup fresh-squeezed lemon juice
6 egg yolks
1 1/2 sticks of butter, melted

Lemon and yolks beaten and whipped together. Then put in the top of a double boiler constantly stirring and then slowly drizzle in the melted butter until you have sunny perfection.

Once brunch was over and presents exchanged, I had a request for my family. I asked them to put their hands on my belly and give thanks to my uterus. I told them, "We wouldn't all be here together if it wasn't for this mighty organ inside me. And now it has to go away. It's done all it can do."

How could they deny me on Mother's Day, the day before my hysterectomy? They clustered around me encircling me with their love. I heard them each whispering their gratitude and goodbyes. I closed my eyes, and with the hands of those I love best on my belly, I thanked my uterus for all the love it had brought to my life.

Afterwards, I felt that as a family we had done what we do best, which is pull together, eat really good food, be irreverent, laugh about weird things, and mightily love each other.

Sadie, the wonder dog, still needed a walk. So did Randy and I. The entire next day would be spent inside the hospital so we needed to be out in nature. We needed sunshine and fresh air. We went to the wetlands at Veterans Park. It was a gorgeous day. We strolled amidst birdsong and happy families.

Halfway around the marsh we said hello to a solitary walker, an old man. He nodded and said, "Nice day" as we passed. Then from behind us he added, "Not for me though. I just went to my wife's funeral." What did he say? It was too bizarre. Randy and I mumbled how sorry we were to hear that, and we continued on. We listened to the birds. Randy pointed out all the turtles that were copulating. Neither of us mentioned the poor old man who had buried his wife on Mother's Day.

Now it is the morning of my hysterectomy, this next big thing. I feel oddly ready to commence. I think, *Since I can't go around it, I have to go through it.* I have a whole conversation with myself. It's a pep talk really. I say, *Time to take this trip, good body. I trust in you and in the doctors and all the staff. I trust in this family and community to support me and to hold me in their best thoughts.* And at that very moment of affirmation, I receive an anonymous text from someone sending love and good healing wishes. It was perfect.

On repeat in my brain is St. Julian of Norwich telling me, "All shall be well, and all shall be well and all manner of things shall be well."

—*edited excerpt from journal and CaringBridge, 10 days after diagnosis*

Onset

I am sitting on the side of my bed. It's a gloriously sunny May morning, the day after Mother's Day, and the day of my surgery for a radical hysterectomy. I am alone for the moment in the quiet. In a few hours all that will change. I will be absorbed by a bureaucratic system filled with specially trained clinicians who are procedural, efficient, and mostly sympathetic and kind. I have written in my journal that I am ready to commence but I know nothing about what lies ahead. I have written that I trust in my body. That's what I know. There's so much I don't know.

Throughout the morning, I attended to the tasks as instructed. I showered with a strong, purple antiseptic soap. It was my second shower in less than twelve hours. I had to do the same thing the night before. Apparently I was contaminated in my sleep so I repeat the process in the morning. Both times my belly was coated in a slimy purple film. Both times I turned my back to the shower and let the soap stay in place for three minutes as I imagined removing my uterus, scrubbing the cancer away with an antibacterial frenzy, then replacing my womb so I could get on with my life.

I was instructed not to eat so I am hungry but mostly miss my tea. Surgery isn't until 2:00 p.m. That leaves plenty of time to fret. Plenty of time to be hungry. By the time I am able to eat again my stomach will have shrunk. I will lose five pounds before chemo even begins. But that's a fraction of the weight I will lose in the next eight months.

In a few hours, hours that will pass as if I am watching myself move underwater, swimming through seaweed and water fans, I will be knocked out and strapped down on the operating table as a robotic arm hovers above me, descends, and makes several small incisions in my abdomen. A surgery tech has locked my hips into an awkward position, preventing any movement for the four-hour surgery. The doctor who will operate the robot is kind and compassionate but still machine meets flesh. Through my earphones a meditation will be on repeat. It will play for the duration of my surgery. A nurse will swab blood.

On this day my future is a big question mark. I wonder how I will ever make it through eight months of chemo and radiation. I try not to think too much about the odds of my survival. I don't know anything about the life-long consequences of my surgery and treatment like lymphedema, hernias, neuropathy, and fatigue. I am trying to stay alive so I am prepared to do what I need to do. I don't know how in the near future I will have to resist the inertia of having my happiness tied only to good lab reports and clean CT scans.

I don't know any of the awful things that will happen during my treatment protocol—like the seizure I will have when my brain swells as a result of chemo or how radiation will damage my lymph nodes and leave scar tissue in my vagina. I have no idea how much cancer my surgeon will find when she slices through my abdominal wall and into my pelvic cavity. I don't know if when she cuts away my ovaries, fallopian tubes, cervix, omentum, uterus, and lymph nodes—then packages them in their own small plastic bags so they don't leak cancer into my body—and sends them down the chute of my vagina and off to the lab to be analyzed, if each organ will have aberrant and malignant cells. Which is to say, I don't know what my staging is. I don't know what sex will be like after a hysterectomy. I don't know how my body will recover.

All I know is I am ready to commence. For some reason I am at peace with all I do not know. I am alone on the side of my bed listening to the quiet when my husband comes up to tell me it's time to go.

....

beloved

Will you wait in the dark for me
as I am abiding in the light for you?

You will find me in the fault-lines
on those nights when I break through.

You will float toward me and away,
buoyant in your midnight salty blue

while I am on ground, sky-blinded
this corporeality, my tattoo.

Meditation on Light and Love—Home from Surgery

When my children were young we lived in a big turn-of-the-century home. We had three floors with five bedrooms on the second and third floors. Most of the years Nate, Chelsea, and Luke were on the third floor. Randy and I were on the second floor.

Raising three kids did not come without sleepless nights of worry, challenge, and more worry. I would lie awake in bed, stare up at the ceiling and think of the precious hearts a floor above me. To get back to sleep, I had to give my mind something to do besides fret. Otherwise, it would invent crazy futures for my children because they didn't heed my words to be kinder, get better grades, or eat fewer hot dogs.

I developed a calming meditation during those sleepless nights. I would envision my children asleep in their beds, their bodies surrounded by the white light of my love and protection. This light would grow until it encircled their beds. I would think, *You are encircled with the white light of my love and protection.* The light grew until it filled their room and then the whole house. Eventually I could imagine their whole world, wherever they went and whatever they did, was encircled with my love and protection. I recreated this simple meditation hundreds of times as I raised my family.

Now I am immersed in light. I am healing in the glow of light created by my children, my family, and my community. I feel it around me, comforting me, helping me find my way through the night.

I am filled with the white light of your love and protection.

—edited excerpt from CaringBridge three days after surgery

The Cancer Lexicon—Post-op Appointment

One becomes a quick study once diagnosed with cancer. There is a brand-new vocabulary that includes words one never wanted to have as part of one's lexicon. Words like the disease that infiltrated my body. But also laparoscopic, metastasis, and other words rarely used in poetry. And unknown body parts. I never knew I had an omentum and now I've lost it.

I appreciate that I need to know what I am fighting. And I understand the need to speak the language of the warriors or allies on my side but I also know I am still in shock. Sometimes I am just too overwhelmed and cannot process, think, or communicate. The stress is too great. I am traveling through a foreign land. I am lucky to have compassionate guides and interpreters who speak this language so I use them when I am rendered mute or when the static in my ears is buzzing too loudly for me to hear.

I take in as much information as I can. And when necessary, I shut off and let Ian, my son-in-law who is a doctor, or Chelsea, my daughter who is a nurse, assume the conversation and explain the details to other family members. I also ask them to read the paperwork or (danger, danger) go online and search "uterine papillary serous carcinoma" (UPSC) for which the National Library of Medicine at the NIH site states, " … is an uncommon but aggressive type of endometrial carcinoma with high recurrence rate and poor survival outcomes." See what I mean? It's too much information for me right now.

In this new cancer lexicon I get distracted by a *more subtle* something, like an undertone in the communication. I think there is a message beneath the message. Maybe I am trying to divine something that isn't there. Still, I listen to *the way* the doctor talks, the phrasing, and what is subtle in her voice. One thing I learned quickly is that when the doctor says, "Well, the good news is … " there will be something coming soon that I do not want to hear.

So the good news from my post-op appointment truly is that the cancer has not spread to the lymph nodes. Thank you for not traveling there, cancer. I am glad my uterus was so comfy and cozy that you *mostly* stuck around there.

Here is the part that I would have preferred not to hear. As has been mentioned to me often, uterine papillary serous carcinoma is a particularly aggressive form of cancer. Survival rates change significantly with the staging of this disease. If the cancer is entirely confined to the uterus, survival rates are better. The doctor alludes to this fact.

That is the "more subtle something" I hear in her voice. But the staging and survival rates information is part of what I saw online before I had to close the computer and cry into Sadie's soft fur. Unfortunately, there were cancer cells outside my uterus, in the left fallopian tube and in the pelvic wash. So I am coded at stage three. That delivers me a chemo-radiation-chemo sandwich from the treatment menu.

The plan now is that I will have three three-week cycles of chemo (that's nine weeks) then six weeks of Monday-through-Friday radiation followed by three three-week cycles of chemo. If all goes according to plan that fills my calendar up to the end of November. But that's getting way ahead of myself.

The regimen is intended to knock the cancer cells out and not allow them to return, the big concern with uterine serous carcinoma. The first three years are the most common for a recurrence. The cancer can recur anywhere: my lungs, my liver, or my vagina. Gasp. Sigh. But again, I am getting way, way ahead of myself.

Randy looked dazed as he added up the weeks, well, months of my treatment plan. But I feel … hmmm … I'm not sure what I feel. Surprisingly, it is not the paralyzing desperation I would have thought—not yet. I feel better knowing what I am facing.

I am still planning to enjoy summer. I am going to continue to appreciate the blessings of people who love me and whom I love more in return. I am going to face what comes.

My biggest challenges will be emotional and mental. My body is so strong and flexible—Thanks, yoga! I think it will do what it has to do. But I will have to monitor the sails of my emotions. Man, I wish I had paid more attention when we had that sailboat.

I am feeling more present than I have since my diagnosis twenty days ago. It has been a whirlwind. I know I cannot escape the storm swirling around me but I hope to find a place in it where I can be calm. I am on the lookout for it. I imagine I will find it and lose it many times over the next eight months. That's okay. I know I have allies who will help me relocate it when I get bumped off-course or when my sails go flat or when the wind is completely gone.

And that is truly the good news.

—edited excerpt from CaringBridge 20 days after diagnosis

Here in this ocean of dreams there be monsters

I Am Always Practicing—First Chemo

Oh, blessed be. Finally a self I recognize. I can stand upright with my shoulders back, not hunched over a very sore tummy. I can sit upright for an hour! I can also drink tea again. I wasn't able to drink tea after chemo! Of all the cruelties (and I have experienced a few) no tea-love is high on the list. These may seem like such small gains. But they are oh-so-significant to me.

I was in a chemo cloud from day two to day ten after my treatment. It was varying degrees of yuck. From physically ill to a weary fatigue that felt like triple or quadruple gravity weighing down on me. I was laid pretty low. It took a visit from Nurse Chelsea (thank you for your career choice, Daughter) to get my nausea under control. It was grueling. Besides several pounds, I lost at least twenty-four hours in a vomitous blur. I threw up so much, my incisions from surgery were raw and aching. I thought I might come apart at the seams. There were also blinding headaches, dizziness, flu-like symptoms, body aches, depression, and complete inertia.

As the days moved on there were bright moments, and I tried hard to realize that after the worst was over, I felt a little better, a little more familiar each day. But there was an alien in my body.

This past Saturday was a day of rain and thunder. I couldn't get out of my own cloudy place. I was especially frustrated. I was tired of being sick and sick of being tired. It's been a month after all. I was feeling alone and sorry for myself, which wasn't helpful to healing or moving forward on the daunting path before me.

In desperation I made a pact with myself—go to the mat. That's all. I didn't tell myself to do yoga or try a few poses. I didn't say, "Breathe." I just made a pact to go every single day. I promised myself that if I only made it to the yoga mat I didn't need to do anything else. I could just lie there. It was like the AA pledge. One day at a time.

So every day now I am on the mat. And generally once there I move into asana, into breath, into my body. It feels both foreign and familiar. This is my body. I have to admit I am really fond of it. I love it so much even in its transformed place. Body and I are on this journey together—practicing wholeness, beginning anew.

Now when I move into warrior pose it has a whole new meaning. I feel my lymph nodes (and their missing sisters) cry out a bit. But a cry turns to a sigh soon enough. Sometimes my body remembers its strength, resilience, and even patience.

I am not starting over exactly but the spiral has swung me around. It has reminded me that I just need to keep on practicing. That is what yoga has taught me. We are all practicing. We are all beginners. And what I see now is how the beginner's mind might be my salvation. It is beautiful; it's open and alive to nuances that my veteran mind might have missed.

So I am stretching. Stretching to understand but also stretching to let go of understanding. Sometimes my muscles shake. Sometimes I tremble on one leg. And sometimes I stand in warrior pose feeling as brave as I have ever felt.

—edited excerpt from CaringBridge 11 days after first chemo

The Abyss

My hair began to fall out on Saturday, June 14, right before noon. It was like I had an appointment with baldness. How bizarre is that? To have a time so specific to begin this thing I have been dreading since I first learned about the Paclitaxel and Carboplatin cocktail that would be careening through my system.

On that day I had lunch scheduled with a group of women friends. We called ourselves the Sistren. Like brethren but female. It was another rainy, stormy, gray day. I felt unglamorous and frumpy. I was soon meeting with the beautiful and artistic Sistren. And I was still wearing the same stretched-out, old yoga pants! I thought I could at least do something with my hair. I had a little pomade on my fingers and I went to spike up my newly shortened tresses. But then … damn it! I had a big hank of hair in my fingers. There were thirty-two of those cute silvery, brown-golden sparkly threads littering my sink. They left behind thin spots on my head, foreshadowing what was to come.

The weather was dreary. My heart was breaking and I couldn't seem to get a full-enough breath. My only consolation was that I had these women to whom I knew I could lament. If I had asked, they would have keened with me. Maybe I should have asked. Instead I joked about it as best I could. And they served me a lunch that not only sustained me but nurtured me spiritually, too.

That is not to say I wasn't terribly *sad* about the hair loss. I was **sad** in large bold print. I knew it was inevitable—but still. I knew it would grow back—but still. I knew it was only hair, but it was my hair. My hair that for fifty-seven years I had been able to take for granted would grow right out of my head. Plus I had just paid forty dollars eight days earlier to have it cut and coiffed. It was my first short haircut since the early nineties. Sweetly, my son, Luke, had told me the style made me look like Charlize Theron. I was just getting used to my short hair. Now I would have to get used to no hair. Bald. No one would mistake me for Charlize Theron.

Now I have all these emotions. I am experiencing a lot of emotional fallout since all my reproductive organs were removed. Before the hysterectomy there may have been only a trickle of estrogen and a whisper of progesterone but there was some. Now there is none. The hormonal change is the cherry on top of the cancer-hysterectomy-chemo sundae. More sighing ensues and often tears.

But I have slept well for the past several nights. What a difference that makes! As always, the love and care from friends and family mean so much. I have had care packages and gifts of scarves, food, cards, texts, and hugs. All these wonderful gifts of spirit strengthen and fill me up. They convince me that I am not alone even though the journey is mine to walk.

That's not to say I haven't had bad days. Of course I have. I have cancer. I am going through chemo; now I have lost my hair. I find I don't look super sexy bald.

But here's the deal. The abyss is always at my feet. If I slip a bit, okay. I let myself feel it. I experience anxiety, sadness, guilt, confusion, and frustration. Sometimes I cry. But that abyss is infinitely deep. The further I slip, the harder it is to climb out. So I try to honor the shadowy places of this journey. There is no glory in denial. But all the while I am working to get myself back to the light. It's better to do yoga, meditation, qigong. Better to laugh. Better to talk with friends. Better to spontaneously spend the night in the woods. It's all therapeutic, like little lifelines to pull myself out of the great abyss.

—edited excerpt from CaringBridge 33 days after first chemo

Upside Down

Something that has been on my mind a lot lately is how after my cancer diagnosis the roles in my family shifted and turned upside down overnight. I found myself dangling from my heels with the blood rushing to my head as Nate, my older son, took over the family dinner night, Chelsea escorted me to myriad doctor's appointments and CT scans, and Luke, my youngest, brought us gigantic aluminum-wrapped trays of food.

The kids divvied up chores; they ran simple errands like buying dog food or shopping for the loose pajama pants I needed as I healed from surgery. They have walked me. They have driven me. They have gathered around me like an insulating force.

Through their efforts the family kept humming along as I took a back seat in an infusion chair. In my addled, chemo-brain daze I heard the melody, a three-part harmony. It was a familiar tune, not exactly lilting, but, at least, it wasn't a dirge. I realized I knew this song well. It was the not-so-simple care and feeding of a sick mother.

For the time being, cancer has inverted the parent-child relationship and I catch myself remembering how much care my mother needed. It doesn't seem that long ago that I was the sole child within my mother's reach and her primary caretaker. Throughout her last twenty years and the especially hard, final two years, I took on more and more as she could do less and less. It was rewarding and exhausting. I never regretted it. It never occurred to me that I would be in my children's life in this worrisome way, not even temporarily.

But now on Friday nights, when I am well enough, we go to Nate's house to eat his roasted veggies and savory meats, always delicious. We leave before the dishes are even cleared. Before cancer, on the rare occasions when I didn't host, I would never have shown up empty-handed. I would never have left before the dishwasher was loaded and counters wiped down.

Earlier this week, Luke just "stopped over" with a pan of lasagna from a small Italian eatery. He walked in and stuck it in my freezer saying matter-of-factly, "For whenever you need it, Ma." As if he just happened upon an abandoned pan of lasagna that desperately needed a home. I was doing him a favor really, taking it off his hands this way.

Chelsea gets an extra burden of being the nurse-daughter. Plus she is married to a doctor. So she receives the calls about my symptoms, interprets doctors' orders, explains neutropenia, and is my medical go-between. She talked at length with the social worker and rounded up a variety of resources for me from home-delivery meal plans, to support groups and grants to help with our medical costs.

Not that long ago, the first thing my kids did upon entering my home was to look in the fridge for something to sample. They would casually open up containers of leftovers, tasting and wondering if I might make them a sandwich. Now, they stuff the refrigerator with ready-to-eat items. Now, they are compelled to put something by in my freezer.

I'm grateful to be on their minds. Glad that I have the luxury of their worry and concern. But I will be ready when we are flipped back around to a more familiar hierarchy.

For now they call to ask, "Need anything from the store, Mom?" "Did you do yoga today?" Or I get their texts, "Love you, Mommy" or "Just thinking of you, Mom." They send me their hope and steadfast love in little emojis: Pink hearts, flowers, and bright smiley faces.

Once upon a time when my kids were little and I was going to live forever, I made lunches for their school day. Each night before bed I packed three brown paper bags full of all the good stuff that would sustain them throughout the day. I put in apple slices, some chips, and smeary peanut butter and raspberry-jam sandwiches wrapped in wax paper. And finally, before I folded up the edges of the paper bag, I slipped in little handwritten notes. Just scraps of paper that said, *I love you; I miss you*—something that connected us while we were apart. A way to let them know they were always in my heart.

Unclenching—Second Chemo with a Side of Neulasta

I received my second round of chemo yesterday after two abortive attempts. Previously my neutrophils (an essential part of the immune system) were too low. I would have had a risk of getting sick (on top of cancer and sick with chemo). Yesterday they were still low but had crept up. The nurse said she would have to get chemo approved. I said, "Tell them I am READY." I felt impatient to keep on track with the chemo schedule. After an hour of waiting, they approved me. They administered extra anti-nausea medication. That may help me the first two nights. Those were worst for the nausea last round. My doctor also prescribed a shot called Neulasta. It will encourage my bone marrow to produce neutrophils. Neulasta has to be given twenty-four hours after chemo. I was allowed to bring it home even though it is an expensive shot since I have a nurse-daughter. They approved Chelsea to stick it to me and boy, did she! It causes bone pain and flu-like feelings—a double shot of chemo with a chaser of yuck.

All in all, I am feeling spiritually and emotionally well. My energy level is low. That is challenging. I still want my go-go-go, to be able to do-do-do but, of course, this is a lesson in be-be-be. I'm learning. I need a perspective overhaul. This is a *big* paradigm shift. Life isn't normal. Or I have a new normal. With that in mind I am turning the volume down on expectation. There is a Buddhist thought that goes something like this: Desire is not the problem. It is the grasping after that is problematic. How I interpret that is this: When my hand is tightly clenched around a notion of myself, I need to loosen. Then I can see a whole new me, waiting to emerge. If I am not clenching, I may open to reveal a new beautiful self.

—edited excerpt from CaringBridge one day after second chemo

Survival Tactics—On the Use of Mantras and Making Awful Statistics Work in My Behalf

I want to tell you about my mantras. Call them what you like. Companion thoughts. Affirmations. Prayers. Besides sending positive thoughts out into the infinite spectrum,

I see my mantras as an alliance between my body, mind, and spirit. My mind wants to fret. My spirit wants to accept. My body wants to heal. Repeating mantras brings those all together for me. It gives my mind something on which to focus when it is pacing and nervous. It hums along with spirit. It sends the right message to body.

This is not to say that I think my thoughts can kill or cure me. I do not. I do not believe that I thought my way into cancer. I do not believe that I can think my way out of cancer. I think of cancer like forces of nature. There are sometimes freak, random storms. I think of mantras like a tool, say, a good umbrella or even a cellar in which to cower and wait out the storm.

A friend was having a bad several days so I shared with her my favorite, simplest mantra and it is this: **I have all I need**. I believe it is the base chakra mantra. And, in essence, it is the most basic truth. I have always had all I needed. I still have all I need. There is much superfluous but in my heart I know **I have all I need**. My friend in turn reminded me of the mantra I used so much in the beginning of my cancer journey: **All shall be well, all shall be well and all manner of things shall be well**. Thank you, Mother Julian of Norwich. And I sent back to my friend the Quaker belief: **The way will open**.

Now I have one more important mantra that I have added to my toolbox. This one comes from my sister. It's a real gift that I am not sure she knew she gave me. That's my favorite kind—straight from the heart without ribbon or expectation. She had told me this several times. It took me awhile to let it sink in. She told me, "You have every reason to believe you will be in that thirty percent."

Wow. The thirty-percent survival rate for my cancer really dogged me early on in my journey. I hated it. I could not look at those studies or think *thirty* percent. I wanted better odds. But now I have a new mantra, a new way to make peace with that statistic. I am going to claim it—make it my own. So I added it to the list. I am sending this message to my body, mind, and spirit.

I have all I need. And I have every reason to believe I will be in that thirty percent.

—edited excerpt from CaringBridge three days after third chemo

We are

closer now like the letters
of a word, or the lines in a poem.

Our bodies are mapping
a future unknown to us.

Together, separate.

Things mutate, solar systems
fluctuate. We can man our vessels.
We can chart our course. But
no one guarantees arriving alive.

We are now no longer just
growing older. Some cells go quiet
while others are bolder.

Two opposing directions
coexist inside me. I can hold
them up in a bright, clear light.

Or I can nestle against them in
a dark, muted sky. Inside me

they beat like Siamese-twin hearts.

The first on a terrestrial, familiar path;

the other, breathless among
the cold and distant stars.

It has never been mine to decide.

Giving Comfort—for the Woman in the Chair

Today I went back to the wig shop. I needed another little bamboo hat. The wig shop was the only place I found that carries them. The hats are soft, comfortable, and easily adaptable. It is important to have a breathable softness against my bald head.

It was weird to be back at the store. It had been a lonely experience my first time there. I was a neophyte to the crushing grind of cancer. I don't know why I went alone. I felt pitiful and the idea of a wig felt shameful. Like something very unpleasant I had to endure, like a colonoscopy. I had sat in the parking lot trying to catch my breath. I was steeling myself, building up my courage to face this cold splash of reality, the stranger in the mirror, a vision of me/not me for the next six to seven months.

Today, I was the veteran with surgery and three chemos under my belt. I hopped out of my car without a thought about the image in the mirror. I knew what was in it. I just wanted a hat. The proprietor had a new customer in the chair—the dreaded wig-fitting chair. I had a flashback to when I sat in that chair, forcing myself to look in the mirror. It was not even two months earlier. It felt like a lifetime ago. The owner asked me if I would talk with the woman in the chair. What could I offer? My heart went out to her. She was younger than I am and with her mother. She was so sad. Her eyes kept filling with tears, brimming over as we talked. I told her she was brave. And she will be beautiful throughout. I gave her my contact info and all the love my heart could offer.

But I wanted to do so much more. I wanted to wrap her in my arms and cuddle her like a baby. I wanted to reach out and catch her tears. I wanted so much to take her pain away, to lighten her new burden. But all I could really do was share my experience. Get her to laugh a little. Tell her how I kept discovering a new normal and that the blow hurts less and less with every day.

As I drove away I kept thinking about how badly I had wanted to comfort her, to nurture and mother her. And I thought *like a great mother*. But what I really meant was like a **Great Mother**. I wanted the spirit of all mothers to come through me just as this great motherlove has come through so many in my community as they have loved and supported me.

Now I see it hurts on the other side of the cancer fence. That feeling a need to comfort can be painful. I am so grateful to the many people, beautiful men and women, who bravely found ways to comfort me. Because giving comfort sounds simple but often it isn't. We think we don't know what to say or do. Being on the receiving end has shown me that almost anything can make a big difference. Chicken noodle soup, a foot massage, daffodils, or just the words, "I'm sorry you have to go through this" can transform a horrible day into one that feels just a bit closer to normal life. Putting love into action makes the journey less lonely for all of us—the giver and the receiver.

I hope the woman in the chair finds her Great Mother love, too. I send mine out to her even though I don't remember her name. I see her filled with love, growing stronger, overcoming despair, putting the days and trials behind her. I see her one day extending her hand to a stranger whose eyes are filling with tears. She feels like it is not enough but she tells her, "It will get easier. You will have a new normal. You are beautiful and brave and strong."

—edited excerpt from CaringBridge 11 days after third chemo

....

Sparring With Radiation

I may have been way too optimistic going into radiation. I thought I was going to dance through it. I thought it would be easier than chemo. Did I say dance? More like a boxing match. Even though I am only one week into radiation I feel like this fight can be called. Here I am knocked out on the mat. And look, the referee is holding radiation's arm up in victory.

The medical team prepped me about potential symptoms that may appear after *three* weeks of radiation. I thought that implied almost three weeks of little or no side effects. Not so. The evening of day one I got sick and went from sick to sicker for days two, three, and four. Finally, on day five, I started to bounce back a bit.

I am going to focus on the bouncing back part. I have one week completed, five weeks to go. I am looking forward to crossing the visits off the calendar. But still the only way through this for me is to focus on the day-to-day. I cannot look too far into the future.

I am in the here and the now. My stomach is back and forth with calm and agitation. But I am not passing out. Who knows what other good things are happening inside my body? Maybe my eyebrows are growing, ready to sprout forth any day now. You know and I know this much: Anything is possible.

—edited excerpt from CaringBridge one week after radiation begins

Closing the Chapter on Radiation

I went into radiation so hopeful. I thought it would be a break from chemo and that I would feel so much better. But in the book of *Jeannie's Cancer Journey,* radiation was my least-favorite chapter. In fact there may have been a time or two when I simply wanted to close the book altogether. That is really not my style. I am generally a finisher when it comes to books.

Although no one pointed it out, I whined a lot during my radiation phase. It was mostly those unavoidable sighs of exhaustion, the moans and groans of carrying around what felt like fifty-pound weights everywhere I went. Once again, I found myself sick and tired. Literally sick and tired. I was nauseated right out of the radiation starting gate and continued to be constantly sick to my stomach for five weeks—nauseous, gassy, and phlegmy. I realized about week three that when they had told me I would experience fatigue they didn't mean really, really tired. They meant a condition unlike any tiredness I have ever known. What they didn't tell me was radiation fatigue would make me feel bereft, like I had a complete lack of will.

It was especially difficult when Randy went to New York for four nights to be with his brother, John, who was very ill from his cancer treatment. I understood Randy's need to go but my diminished state made me cower at the thought. I tried to put aside the anxiety of being alone. It was only four days but my radiation weariness was all-consuming. I was shaky, disoriented, and couldn't hold food down. The toll radiation was taking on me left me debilitated and vulnerable. Thankfully my kids each volunteered to spend one night with me. Just to know someone was there felt like a life preserver had been tossed my way. It wasn't exactly a pajama party but it kept me intact and on track.

So I did, in fact, complete my chapter on radiation. Monday was my final appointment down in the basement of the hospital behind the nine-inch-thick doors in a room the size of a closet, all alone except for the radiation beams. I am grateful for all those who helped me keep the book open.

I am thrilled to be finished with my six-week sentence but I will miss the radiation techs. It is one of those weird twists in life that some of the loveliest people work in such a horrible environment. All my techs were sweet, compassionate, and wholly present in their jobs. I am thankful for them. Although I will miss them, I can live my life contentedly never seeing them again.

One thing that helped me get through radiation was that I had the most amazing Girl Party about halfway through it. Dear friends of mine organized it for me. It was a halfway-through-treatment-and-good-bye-to-my-girl-parts party. It was wild and loving and sweet and imaginative—everything I could have hoped for in a girl party. So many fabulous, strong, loving, beautiful women attended. Oh, and great food. And because of some unknown benevolence, I actually felt mostly well that day. I partied with my tribe, toasting the day with my non-alcoholic sparkling wine! And now I have an altar filled with seashells, rocks, bowls, meditation balls, angel cards, poems, hearts, trinkets, and more. All of these mementos of love and strength remind me on a daily basis that I am indeed surrounded by a powerful healing community.

Also, on a positive note (it's always good to note the positive), it's been awhile since I had chemo so my hair follicles are pushing up sprouts. Little tiny hairs are growing out all over my body. My favorite regrowth happens to be my eyebrows and eyelashes! They are pretty awesome. I missed them terribly so I find myself petting them often, pointing them out to people and admiring them in the mirror while saying, *Hello, darlings, welcome home.* The hair on the top of my head is growing in a bit, too. It's all salt-and-pepper and still too short to go about without a hat. My head gets too cold. Who knew how insulating hair was! It's nice to see the regrowth. I know all these lovely hairs will fall out with the next chemo but I am appreciating them in the here and now.

Now I get an actual break from cancer treatment. My oncologist originally said four to six weeks. I will have an appointment with her soon for assessment. I will have another CT scan so they can see what's going on inside me. And then they will schedule the rest of chemo. Just typing the words "four-to-six-week break" makes me giddy. I can't imagine what it will be like to have four weeks without treatment. It sounds wonderful.

I'm sure I'll think back on my radiation treatment and remember a chapter of which I was not at all fond. But I know it's an important part of my story. I'm glad I didn't put the book down or tear out the pages in exasperation. I read every word. And now I turn the page. The story moves forward. Here I go.

—edited excerpt from CaringBridge six weeks after radiation began

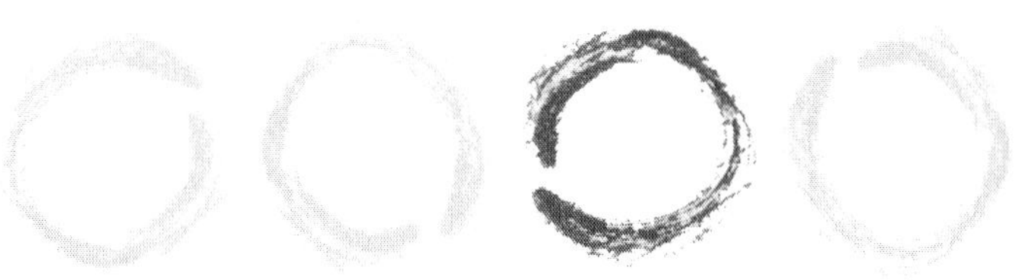

I am floating above them

My Mysterious Brain

With cancer there are no clear or easy answers. So it's the same with cancer treatment. The list of possible side effects that they hand out isn't exhaustive, exclusive, or a guarantee. And what happens to one person won't necessarily happen to another. Some treatments cause horrible side effects. Some are barely a snag in the cancer patient's routine.

No one could have predicted what ensued two days after my fourth chemo. The doctors still aren't sure. I think my brain took a much-needed time-out on Sunday. My poor brain may have felt like seven months is just a really long time to be constantly recalibrating, adjusting, and making sense of the spectrum of disease.

I was standing next to the dining room table by a chair. We had just hooked up the IV fluids that keep me hydrated after chemo and turned on the drip. I said to Randy, "I don't feel well" and then collapsed in the chair beside me. I was completely nonresponsive. But, weirdly, even though I couldn't speak, I was cognizant the whole time. I just couldn't move, speak, or respond in any way. I was out for seven or eight minutes. My eyes were fixed all the way to the right and then after a few minutes they closed, which worried Randy even more. I could hear him asking me to look at him. I could hear him calling Chelsea on the phone, then, when she didn't answer, calling 911 and talking to the dispatcher. At one point the dispatcher told him to get me out of the chair and lay me down on the floor. Randy tried to pick me up and I thought to myself, "What's wrong with him? Why is he picking me up so weirdly?" Then I realized it was because I was like a bag of rags. Once I was on the floor I started to emerge from my brain time-out. I could speak again. My tailbone hurt against the hardwood floor and I said "Ouch." Randy was still on the phone with the dispatcher. My leg was twitching and I wanted him to tell the dispatcher that so I kept saying, "Involuntary movements, involuntary movements."

I was whisked away in all the flashing lights of the ambulance. I am sure it caused a sensation on our block. Once at the ER the doctor and the neurologist couldn't agree on what transpired, much less what caused it. Was it a seizure? Or was it low blood pressure and dehydration? We don't know. But I passed all the neurological testing, which, considering I had major chemo brain, was pretty impressive. I knew the month, where I was, what happened, and I could even remember the three words the doctor told me to remember. Randy did, too, by the way.

I had to have another CT scan *(Hello, old friend)* and then because the CT scan wasn't conclusive, an MRI. Cue the *Jaws* soundtrack. This insidious test and I are not on friendly terms. Years ago when I had a herniated disk, I had to have a couple of MRIs of my back. I hated them but that was nothing compared to the MRI of my head. But to recap, I had just had chemo two days before. I was in the throes of chemo nausea and exhaustion. I was dizzy and achy. I had just had a weird and disturbing brain incident, plus I am highly claustrophobic so, sure, lay me out on a slab, screw a cage over my head, and put me in a confined tube for thirty-three minutes with what sounds like demons playing loud, clanging electro-metal music while simultaneously banging on the outside of the tube. It's the Murphy's rule of cancer: Just when you think your situation is precarious, it will get worse.

The creepiest part was when they placed the cage over my head. They even screwed the cage down to the table. I get the chills just writing "cage on my head." I had asked for Valium, which they were happy to provide. Once I was doped up as much as they would allow, Randy sat at my feet so I would feel less alone as I was enveloped by the dark tunnel of the MRI.

I could feel the nausea, the anxiety, and the fear battling it out with the Valium. I did my best to find my calm, and I managed to lie still for thirty-three minutes by thinking of all the things I loved. At one point toward the end of the MRI I mistakenly opened my eyes because I thought it was over. I saw the tube right above my head (how one might envision being inside a casket) and the cage over my face and just thought, *This is some crazy shit.* Then I closed my eyes and went through my list of all the beloved elements that make up my life.

So now I wait for a follow-up with neurology. My oncologist is concerned because the MRI showed an enhancement in the meninges. Surprisingly, the meninges are not one of the final frontiers in *Star Trek* but the lining that encloses the brain and spinal cord. *An enhancement in the meninges.* It could be a cloaked Klingon vessel armed and ready to fire. It could be a lump or it could be nothing at all. That pretty much sums it up in the extreme sport of cancer.

Here's what I think about the enhancement: At closer examination they will see it's a tiny Post-it® note. In lovely script it reads, "Dear Cancer, Chemo, Radiation, and Worry: All right, already. You've made your point. Your days are numbered. We are going to be fine without you. Love, Jeannie's Mysterious Brain."

In the meantime I am coping with the chemo effects from chemo date number four. I am emerging from the nausea. Dizzy, lightheaded, exhausted, and weary seem to be the adjectives this go-round. Oh, and the bone pain—all the long bones in my leg—my hips, knees, and ankles are throbbing. But my body seems much friendlier to food this time. If it weren't for the curious, mysterious brain incident on Sunday I would say this was one of the easier chemos. Wait, did I just write that? Easy chemo, really? Funny how perspectives change.

—edited excerpt from CaringBridge one week after fourth chemo

Ambiguity and Restriction

Absurdity often arises with the unknowns of cancer treatment. I was relaying the story of trying to solve the mystery of my recent brain episode to my friend, Flo. After I finished telling her the end result of my visit with the neurologist, she replied, "So basically you came away from the appointment with ambiguity and restriction." The story of my cancer journey! But it sounded like a chapter heading, and so it is.

I was fully ready to leave my curious, mysterious brain incident behind me. Some things are better left unexplained. I didn't feel the need to fully understand what happened. More mystery, please! Keeping in mind, of course, that mystery is very different from ambiguity. But as anyone who has had a chronic or life-threatening illness knows, one event can send you down a path where the mire just gets muddier. And sometimes that mire is BS. (I was going to add in a gyre sucking me into the mire but—whoa—the word sounds were too much like a Jules Verne fantastical drama.)

My oncology doctor wanted me to follow up with a neurologist about the "enhancement" on the MRI. So I did. Imagine my surprise when the neurologist wouldn't even speak about the MRI or the enhancement. He said that was an oncology question which, of course, would refer me back to the doctor who referred me to the neurologist. *Please step this way into your personalized mire, Ma'am.* He went on to say that the enhancement could be cancer cells *(Please don't say that)* or it could be a minor infection that might even be resolved already. This doc had no sense of humor so I didn't bother asking him if I got to choose because I was fairly certain which one I would prefer.

This neurologist's mission was finding the *cause* of my mysterious brain incident. And this guy was serious. Like looking deep-into-my-eyes-for-the-answer serious. He asked me a bunch of questions and ran me through some manual exams. After touching my nose with eyes closed, walking toe-to-heel forward, walking heel-to-toe backward (all things you might see drunk people doing on the side of the road), I told him I thought I did pretty well and now could we test Randy? The doctor stared at me like my question itself was an indication of something he could uncover. Like maybe a sense of humor?

In the end, the doctor was quite certain that I had, in fact, had a seizure. He said that people who faint don't do the weird eye thing or have a loss of consciousness for as long as I did. So now I have to have a three-hour EEG on Friday and an echocardiogram. Mire, mire, mire.

The echocardiogram is to rule out any heart issue that may have contributed to the mysterious brain incident—something like a minor stroke. This is unlikely and again the test is to rule it out. The EEG is to determine if my brain is having any other seizure-like activity.

Now for the restriction: As a result of this neurology visit I cannot legally drive for three months. That is three months from the time of the seizure. Man, this whole cancer thing is really cramping my style.

So in summary, I didn't get any definitive answer about the enhancement on my MRI, plus, as a bonus gift: No driving for three months. In essence, ambiguity and restriction.

I know I can deal with this. I'm very experienced now dealing with constantly shifting realities. I am adept at inconvenience, humiliation, deprivation, and obstacles. What's a little no-driving restriction besides a complete lack of independence and my personal freedom? I will need to enlist more help now, such as rides to acupuncture, doctor appointments, and the store.

As I have seen throughout this journey, people with cancer do not get a pass from other life challenges. For us the extra challenges recently have been particularly devastating. Randy's brother, John, died from glioblastoma. He faced the horrible diagnosis with both grit and tender appreciation for all the love that surrounded him. From the outset the prognosis was dim. He had an unlikely chance of survival but still maintained a sense of peace. Inevitability does not make the loss less painful for those who loved him. He was a good man, sweet and kind. He will be missed.

And now, for some reason, our dog, our reliable companion for the past thirteen years, has stopped eating. Sob. I've had to ask myself, *Is it because of all the tears that I spilled into her soft brown fur?* We spent a couple hours at the vet figuring out she was in incredible pain from arthritis and who knows what else. Something (maybe freezing-cold walks on ice) must have triggered a bad episode or a break for her. She is on pain pills and anti-inflammatory drugs. And I am staying close by, reciting my mantras over and over to her.

But now comes Thanksgiving with its reminder of gratitude served up right next to mashed potatoes and gravy. It is our family's highest holy day. It will be mighty, mighty in this house. As I have been prepping this week, I have thought about all the years we have spent around this old oak dining room table. My family has logged twenty-three years around this table's honey-hued wood—laughing, loving, laughing, feasting, drinking, loving, and laughing.

I remember buying this table new in 1991. It was a major purchase for us. The delivery men brought it in off the truck and set it up for us. It was a mini-event. I'm sure I was planning the celebratory dinner in my head when one of the men said to me, "Do you think this is the last table you will ever buy?" It was an odd, almost-prophetic question. It has stayed with me all these years because it was a magical moment for me. I knew the answer right then and there. *Yes, this table would be the last table we would ever buy.* It was our family's table.

Next week on Thanksgiving Day we will all be around this table heavy with abundance. We will be together in our battered or brand-new baby bodies, with our tested and transformed hearts, in our mystery and even our ambiguity. We will raise our glasses, remember those we have lost, bless our food, and love this moment of our thanksgiving.

—edited excerpt from CaringBridge two weeks after fourth chemo

. . . .

Chemo Slipped Out When No One Was Looking

Today was technically my last chemo! I know, I am surprised, too. Here is the very long story made a bit shorter—the condensed version.

"Enhancement" seen on MRI = swelling of my brain caused by Carboplatin, one of my nasty and effective chemo drugs. Swelling on brain = seizure. EEG shows likelihood of more seizures. Result: Temporary prescription to anti-seizure + no driving until February 9 = antsy Jeannie. Risk from Carboplatin + brain swelling > prophylactic benefit of final chemo = no sixth chemo. (Obviously I am a terrible mathematician. Why I would use this as a literary technique is beyond me but take this into account: I had chemo all day and lots of drugs, it's 10:33 p.m. and I have had little sleep, so there it is.)

I began this journey on May 2, seven months ago. After surgery, three rounds of chemo, six weeks of daily radiation, and two more rounds of chemo, I am finished with my treatment protocol. I wanted to complete all six rounds of chemo because I like to complete what I set out to do but I also feel compelled to keep my brain healthy.

My oncology doctor was ready to call it quits even on today's chemo (the fifth) but weirdly enough I advocated for it. I was ready. My neutrophils weren't ready. They were low. But not so low that I couldn't talk my doctor into letting me proceed. So I had my final chemo, final Neulasta. Hopefully, there will be no more seizures.

Now I enter the observation period. I will have a CT scan in January. Then another MRI (shudder) and EEG in February. After that I will have checkups with my oncologist every three months for two years, then every six months for three more years.

For the last several months my mantra has been that I am healing with Grace, Strength, and Presence. I capitalize them as I would other important trios like the Magi, the Bronte sisters, or the Stooges. I interpret Grace as acceptance rather than the traditional Christian thought of the favor of God. But God's favor works, too, because with acceptance I struggle less and trust more. That feels God-like. Strength is implicit in the challenge, but I am inconsistent. I have to exercise my Strength the way I once lifted weights to keep the arm flab away. Now I work out with Strength to keep away the flab of whininess, despair, and ungratefulness. Lastly, Presence (which might be my favorite part), because why am I doing all of this work if I am not paying attention to life right now? All along I have reminded myself: *I am still living. My life is not on pause.* So amidst the questions, the pain, and heartbreak I am being Present, aka experiencing all the joys of this life I've built.

Lately when I take my walks—often alone now because our dear dog, Sadie, is suffering too, and doing poorly—I call out to the visible and invisible world around me. I call out to my family, my community, to loved ones past, present, and future, to the two-legged, four-legged, the winged and finned, to those resting on clouds, driving in beautiful cars, to animal, vegetable, mineral. I even call out to Melchior, Caspar, and Balthazar; to Charlotte, Emily, and Anne; to Larry, Moe, and Curly: *Hello*, I say, *I'm here. I survived all that was before me. I am healing with Grace, Strength, and Presence.*

—edited from journal and CaringBridge, final chemo

Just Before the Dawn

Randy's brother, John, died of glioblastoma while I was in the home stretch of my treatment protocol. It was a Friday morning in autumn and The Beatles sang *All You Need is Love* from the speaker beside his bed. The two times Randy visited John during my treatment I had been unable to accompany him. Mostly, I was too sick to board a plane, too sick to accommodate the unknowns of travel, but I would have loved to say goodbye in person.

I spoke to John on the phone three days before he passed. As our call was ending, he told me, "Just be grateful for every single day, Jeannie. That's what I am doing. We are so lucky. We have so much love." Simply that.

The morning after John died, Randy and I packed up to go camping. I was a little sick and still weak from the rigors of radiation. I was scheduled to start chemo again in two weeks. This was my break between poisons.

It was just the three of us—Randy and me in varying degrees of brokenness, and Sadie the dog, our constant comfort companion. We drove down Highway 35 on the Wisconsin side of the Mississippi River. The curving road took us through small towns dotted with bakeries and biker bars. We passed a train; later the train passed us. Then we veered away to Perrot State Park. We both sighed as we drove down the dirt road lined with giant trees. It was just what we needed—solitude and nature—the Mississippi River on one side, bluffs rising up before us on the other and a softly darkening sky overhead big enough to hold our broken hearts.

For two days we hiked in the woods, along the river, up the bluffs, and back down. There were a few stragglers of trees with their fall leaves of red and orange and plenty of crunch and color under our feet. Sadie was thirteen, a senior citizen but game for any adventure in the woods. I was weak from chemo and radiation. I had to stop to catch my breath on every uphill hike. Sadie panted and paused along with me. I joked with Randy about his two old ladies.

Mostly we hiked in silence. Sadie out in front, Randy behind her and then me, the slowest of all. We walked in our own thoughts. We talked a little about John, but he was everywhere with us—in the old oaks, at the folksy bar, even in the morning as we lingered over tea and toast.

On our last day of camping, the park was empty. I sat alone on a picnic table in the dappled sun thinking about my brother-in-law. He had an extraordinary capacity to love unconditionally. Like many others, I was drawn to this rare beacon. His illness had been chaotic and his departure abrupt. In less than a year he had gone from injury and confusion to diagnosis and finality. His whole future disintegrated and crumbled before him. I felt caught between his life and mine. The day around me was impossibly beautiful. I sat in the golden autumn light, bouncing back and forth between sadness, hope, and anxiety. His words echoed inside me: *Just be grateful for every day. We are so lucky. We have so much love.*

A few short weeks later, in November, just after my fourth chemo and the seizure, the weather turned dangerously cold. It was a treacherous landscape—ice covered everything. Somehow Sadie suffered an injury. We never knew what had happened.

The X-rays showed a ruinous spine of hairline fractures from arthritis and the wear and tear of thirteen years. We tried pain pills and anti-inflammatories. For a day or two she seemed improved. Then she got worse. For a month we exhausted every option the vet proposed.

In early December I had my fifth, and final, chemo. I was still holding out for a miracle cure for Sadie. But there was no improvement. She continued to decline. She could no longer put any weight on her back legs. We rigged a sling from an old sheet to help her stagger outside to go to the bathroom. Sometimes she would face-plant into the snow.

I knew we were out of options. But still I stretched out beside her on the floor, hand-fed her bits of turkey and begged her to get better. My sadness was as large as a house and filled every room.

It seemed cruel that we would lose Sadie in the midst of all we had gone through. Cruel to say goodbye the week before Christmas and yet, it simply was. I had finally completed my cancer treatment. All the days of 2014 that had once been stacked before me and seemed insurmountable were gone. Everything of that year had finally been emptied out. We could agonize over our losses or we could begin to restore ourselves in the light refracted through our broken hearts. To move forward we had to imagine that the joy of what may come could ameliorate the sorrow left over from our devastating year.

I felt emptied, too, hollowed out yet somehow hallowed as well—like I had survived some purge and was now the most elemental part of myself. At that moment, in the changing of one year into another, nothing in me felt superfluous. I had turned the page. I was ready to begin again in a new dawn. I would fill myself up with the light of it.

All this

> *"… to fall/patiently to trust our heaviness*
> *Even a bird has to do that before he can fly."*
> *—Rainer Maria Rilke*

I walk beside the river rimmed
with ice, a dark thread of mystery.

What flows downstream disappears
from my sight as it joins the greater water.

I think of you when I see the cardinal,
bird of my heart, bright red flash
against the dusky sky.

I think of all that has been unpromised.

Oh, our shattered hearts beating
in their darkness. We've always known
it is not whether they will break but
what we do with their brokenness.

So I say, thank you, broken heart
who like an egg is just fragile,
brittle beauty until broken.

Thank you, broken heart, cracked
with all this glorious light pouring in;
cracked with all this glorious life
blossoming out.

All this glorious life.

The Art of Levitation

Six weeks after the completion of my eight-month cancer treatment protocol, I had a follow-up CT scan and blood work. These post-treatment tests were to see if—besides making me sick, inert, and leaden—chemo and radiation had fulfilled their job descriptions.

Of course, after the tests I entered the dreaded waiting period for the results. Waiting can be so ponderous. Three days can seem interminable. I tried to remember that I was living, not just waiting. But the mind so easily falls into that bad-habit rut of worry. It wants to work that groove into infinity. Luckily, I had prearranged outings and company so I wasn't just sitting on my couch coping with an acute case of scanxiety.

The day before my doctor's appointment I received a test result electronically through MyChart. I had decided earlier that if results came through before my appointment I would not look at them. I would wait for the conversation with my doctor. I had journeyed enough in the cancer territories to know how badly I can misconstrue medical information without proper explanations. If there was anything negative in the test results I wanted to have my doctor talk me through it before I fell down a rabbit hole of worst-possible outcomes.

But just knowing results were there at my fingertips began to whittle away at my decision and at my calm. I debated back and forth about checking the numbers and seeing the radiologist's report. But I persevered and went to my yoga mat instead. I did fifty minutes of focused yoga and ten minutes of meditation. I came downstairs and deleted the message instantly. I never even peeked at it.

After that victory, Randy and I had a beautiful dinner with a dry red wine. Yoga and wine are vastly different but are both great soothers. Throughout dinner we laughed and cried, feeling like we were on the approach of somewhere brand new. Even though it was just another trip to the doctor's office it felt like we were about to explore new lands. We had that exploration anticipation.

Finally, it was the morning of the appointment and we were taking our last sips of tea and walking out the door.

Upon arrival at the clinic we discovered my doctor had been called away for emergency surgery so she wasn't there to give us my results! Yikes—all that waiting and now not-my-doctor stood before me. Instead it was one of the fellows who worked under her. Not fellows like, "Hey, Fellas," but doctor fellows. I had never met this doc before. She wasn't very conversant in giving test-result information. She spoke to us very slowly and without a lot of emotion.

First she told me my CA125, the blood-work marker, was thirteen. Okay, that was good news because anything under thirty is normal. "And then … your scan, she said so s-l-o-w-l-y. I think she was in slow motion really—like a football replay. "Your scan … looks … completely clear."

Wow. Who sighed that enormous sigh? In my memory it was like all the breath went out of the room in one big swoosh. It was exhaled from me, from my husband, from the uncomfortable chairs, the exam table, even the plastic diagram of the reproductive system. Whoosh. Then it came rushing back in, full of oxygen, right into our grateful lungs.

After that there was a lot of breezy, quick talk (showing she can modulate her speech) about the three-month checkup, the MRI to be scheduled, the EEG yet to come, many etcs. I was all smiles and nodding my head to my own internal rhythm. I was present and communicative but I was adrift—floating in the lightness of being me. Not me the patient; not me the sick woman, or the bald one, or the one with no neutrophils. Just me. For a few moments I felt like me.

As we finished up, Dr. Gellar came into the room. I hugged her close and thanked her for all she had done. It felt inadequate. How does one properly give thanks in such a situation? But she hugged me back and reiterated everything in calm, friendly tones, pausing to laugh with me at the wonder of it all.

Then I began to let my family and friends know my results through Facebook, text, and phone calls. My kids had been on pins and needles. I had received many texts and emails early this morning of last-minute good wishes. So I sent out my missives. My glorious "me" good news.

I received back a generous outpouring of love, relief, concern, and **emoticons!** Oh, my gosh, the emoticons: Smiley faces, tears of joy, red hearts, pink hearts, more and more hearts, thumbs up, doggies wagging tails, doggies dancing, foxes, biceps, champagne bottles. Modern pictograph odes of health and happiness.

When I was a teenager my friends and I used to levitate one another. It was a girl thing we did at slumber parties. We would take turns being levitated: One person at the head, two on each side, one at the foot. I don't think we were consistent about anything except for the chant, which was never creepy. Over and over we would incant, "She is light as a feather. She is stiff as a board." Invariably, we would lift our sister-friend by our fingertips and she would be *light as a feather.*

I loved the feeling of levitation—held in faith by these dear friends. I loved the spirituality of it (real or not) and the ritual we shared. We may have shared some other ritualistic substances as well but it was all so innocent. The most important piece in my young mind was this feeling of trust and well-being for the levitated. We were holding her up with our mere fingertips, so really we were holding her up with our connection, with our faith, with our love.

Throughout cancer treatment I experienced many acts of levitation. Over and over those around me—strangers, clinicians, friends, and family transformed me from my dull and leaden state into something I could manage. I was held up by love and goodwill. It made all the difference in the world. It made me *light as a feather.*

—edited excerpt from CaringBridge five weeks after the end of treatment

Shadow and Light

As a Joni Mitchell devotee, I know that shadow and light are not just inherent but essential to every picture. Her lyrics are bouncing around in my head a lot lately. The sun is shining in Minneapolis today which makes shadows dance across my landscape. The light is so very welcome but as I meandered along the creek today I felt myself equally in the shadow even though in my heart I walked in the glory of the sun. It is an apt metaphor, and an apt theme song for me, because literally and figuratively, I am finding my way through both shadow and light in this old-new, new-old body of mine.

After my post-treatment appointment on January 15, I wanted very much just to feel normal. But what is normal now? Or ever, for that matter? As a friend told me, "Normal is a setting on a dryer." So maybe not normal, but I wanted to be back to, or at least in the vicinity of, the old me, the one I was before the intersection of Jeannie and disease, before eight months of treatment for cancer, before the absurdity my life became.

Not so fast, little missy was the response to my little fantasy. Because there's an order to this: First there is the cancer, then there is the treatment, and lastly there is the dealing with effects of cancer and treatment. Just when I thought I would be visiting fewer doctors, rebuilding my strength, toning long-neglected muscles, growing hair, and drinking red wine, I find myself negotiating issues and going right back to seeing way too many doctors, clinicians, and therapists. All right, message received. I am in the sunshine. I am in the shadow. I am in the light. The shadow. The shadow and the light.

You know when you make a major purchase like a car or a refrigerator the sellers always try to upcharge you for an extended warranty? That's what I wanted with my surgery and treatment. I wanted some kind of guarantee that I would be okay for ninety days, six months, twenty years. I would have paid extra for that plan. Big time. But no one offered it to me. And man, I hope I am not a lemon.

In January, just a few days after my post-treatment appointment, I was attempting a twenty-one-day yoga challenge. I was oblivious to the fact I was living in an "old me" fantasy. I was trying to do something that would have been fine before cancer and treatment. But it was too much for this current body. I injured something—my psoas muscle or inguinal ligament. It's unknown. I was in a bit of pain and had some swelling at the leg joint and on the right side of my pelvis. After two to three weeks I called the doctor. My oncologist was concerned when she heard *swelling in the pelvis.* So I was back in the doctor's office getting a manual check and a blood draw. It did not help my mental state when I read about a woman with my diagnosis who had an orange-sized tumor one month after her last CAT scan. Yikes. But luckily there wasn't evidence of a tumor and my CA125 was still the same as it had been the previous month.

But what was going on? My doctor ordered an ultrasound to rule out a deep vein thrombosis. Nothing. Then I noticed my thigh was quite swollen, too. I measured it. It was more than an inch bigger than my left thigh. That made it clear that I was dealing with lymphedema. I had multiple visits to a lymphedema therapist. He said I had more than a liter of extra fluid in my right leg. That is more than two pounds. Poor thigh.

The lymphedema is most likely because of the injury complicated by the removal of sixteen lymph nodes during my surgery and then the radiation therapy. I will probably have lymphedema the rest of my life. There is no cure. It is one of the effects of treatment. It is unpleasant, unpredictable, and uncomfortable but it is not cancer. And for that I am thankful.

As I deal with my colossal leg I get to wear this super-sexy foot-to-thigh compression sock! Randy has never been happier. It's not that bad, really. It's just like my entire leg is compressed, squeezed, tourniquet-ed. But I just repeat to myself, "It is not cancer. It is not cancer." *Shadow and light.*

On the bright side (light, light!) two doctors have released me. I had to have an ultrasound, an MRI, and an EEG to satisfy them but at last the cardiologist, the neurologist, and I have gone our separate ways. I wish them well and hope they get over me quickly.

But I do know that no one gets to buy that warranty plan. We all have a built-in obsolescence. And there will always be newer models. That's life. I am still seeking the light. I will always be a light-seeker but I also know I can make my way through the dark. It's been proven. And while it can be scary it's part of the whole picture.

Randy and I are soon to be embarking on a sojourn south. It is part of our emotional therapy for this year and part of our effort to live more in the light. We will be camping in Bahia Honda State Park about thirty miles north of Key West for two weeks. Yum. All that tropical light. We will take a week to get there visiting several stops along the way including Nashville and St. Augustine. As you can imagine we are so very much looking forward to a break, a vacation, our own little moment in the sun.

—edited excerpt from CaringBridge three months after the end of treatment

A shore of stars sparkling in the sand

Now and Then, Then and Now, Nowthen

There is a city in Minnesota named Nowthen. I have never been there. But I have seen its signs on the highway. It's a funny name. The name is a colloquialism that one of its founders often used. But when I see the sign for Nowthen I imagine a town that is caught between tenses or caught between times. One that is acutely aware of the past while living in the present. A town a bit like me.

In the nine months since completion of my treatment protocol, life is moving onward in a normal*ish* fashion. It's still the *new* normal or again it's a new normal. Because normal keeps picking up the finish line and moving it on me. That's okay. I don't want to finish. We all know where the finish line gets us.

I have noticed some positive transformation taking place. I traveled to Albuquerque in June to visit my sister. I went alone. That may not seem like a big deal for a grown woman, but cancer bestows a bevy of vulnerabilities upon a person. That vulnerability can be weakening as well as illuminating. The weakening includes a general fear, a foreboding that there is imminent danger all around. That's no way to live. And it must be challenged in order to move beyond it.

Once I returned home from the visit I felt like I had advanced a level (just like in a video game) in my life-after-cancer treatment. It is surprisingly hard to get through a day without hearing about cancer. But I was less preoccupied by it. Less often I thought, *Oh but … I have cancer, I might not be here; I am sick*. It was glorious. To get to a place of reprieve is a beautiful thing. I felt such freedom.

Even though I am on this next level and doing my best to live in the Now, I am often reminded of my Then. There is a reason why Now is so challenging. It's because of the Then. The past is nearby whispering to me. In my mind it walks alongside me but for my body it is a long distance—a continent or maybe a solar system away. Old habits are hard to break. My mind wants to run my life currently as if I still have that pre-cancer body. But I don't. I have this one. It is full of limitations. And that makes sense; it has been through hell.

Stress really takes a toll on me now. I used to be able to do so much: Multitask, take care of everyone, do all the things that needed doing, please most everybody (because that was important). But this is where the Now is so very different. Now if I try to do life like that, I get sick. Really sick.

So I am asking myself how do I manage stress now? The cancer counselor tells me I have to put myself first. Well, that's hard. But no one is going to manage my stress for me. So just like I had to do with the medical system, now I have to advocate for myself with the world around me. That's harder than one might think. Maybe even harder than it was with the medical system because then I was so apparently sick. Now I don't look sick but I am clearly on an edge, balancing precariously.

In the last two weeks I had other routine cancer screenings. My mammogram went fine but the colonoscopy was a disaster. I will save the gory details, but after all the prep the doctor was not able to do a regular colonoscopy. I had to go over to another clinic and have a colonography, a specialized CT scan.

The results came back mid-week. There were no signs of cancer in my colon. But there was a spot on my lung—one centimeter. There had been something on my lung last year and the radiologists thought it was probably from an old bout of pneumonia. But there's no mention of an actual size in last year's reports. The lungs happen to be one area in which my cancer likes to recur. I asked my primary doctor about it. He can't see the old films or reports because they are from my oncologist's system and they don't automatically share. I asked my oncologist and she can't see the new radiologist's film because it is in a different system. Hmmm.

So I went into the weekend without any definitive news about the spot. I was in a place of relative calm. But I have also developed a cough. Of course. It's a cold or allergies or pollutants. But this is a great example of life in the NowThen. The cough, even the spot, would just be an irritating nuisance before cancer but in the NowThen it has different implications. Implications that I mostly try to ignore.

The weekend has passed and I still haven't heard back from my doctor. Is no news good news? Or is it just no news? Is it irresponsible of me to publish this post without a definitive answer? One of my most basic desires with my CaringBridge is to share the experience of life with cancer. I am an infinitely curious person. I want to know how others approach challenge, hardship, joy. I hope that is one of the reasons you are on this journey with me, too.

Here is the point I am trying to make. This right here … this waiting, this wondering, this actively, and regularly, putting **it** out of my mind and out of my way, again and again … this is a huge part of life in my NowThen.

I have to keep moving on—pursuing my joys, writing poems, holding my grandbabies, and loving my family and friends. Yes, there are clouds overhead. I cannot deny it but it's like this: Without a little cloud cover, the sun might be blinding. So maybe the clouds actually help me hold my life in fuller view.

To paraphrase Paul Simon, the times are filled with miracle and wonder.

—edited excerpt from CaringBridge nine months after the end of treatment

Cashmere and Dish Soap—Life Beyond Cancer Treatment

One of my biggest struggles with cancer and its after-effects is the uncertainty of life lived after cancer diagnosis. I am often unsteady in my footing, with balance and equilibrium, both literally and metaphorically.

Before cancer I fully intended to, and assumed I would, live a long life. I was going to be that old lady who wore bikini underpants under her granny jeans and smeary black eyeliner on her sparse lower lids. It's not like I planned for life in my nineties; it just was a given in my mindset. A fait accompli handed down from good habits, good genes, and good assumptions.

Now I think about my life in a way I never did before cancer. I feel like I have a tiny, insistent metronome inside me clicking back and forth between sometimes-opposite realities. Or often between narrow differences in perspective. It's going back and forth between what my mind brings up and what I then try to dispel from my mind. Click/clack, click/clack. I am strong/I am sick, I am living life/I am doomed, I am cancer-free/what's that pain in my belly, buy the beautiful cashmere sweater/don't buy the frivolous cashmere sweater.

Two months ago a radiologist discovered that spot on my right lung. The spot was detected because a routine colonoscopy didn't work on my loopy intestines so I had to have a specialized CT scan. There was no evidence of cancer in my colon. Click. But there was this suspicious spot on my lung. Clack. If I had been able to have a normal colonoscopy instead of the CT scan no one would have known about the spot. Was that a good thing or a bad thing? Click/Clack.

What ensued was almost two months of figuring out what was going on in that right lung of mine. I had had a persistent cough since July. And hadn't I noticed some weakness in my lung and shortness of breath upon exertion? I thought I had. Was it an infection? Click. Or was it cancer? Clack. I joked, *hopefully it's just a little TB … anything but cancer.* Click/clack.

After a certain amount of back and forth about the scans (different medical systems have difficulty sharing records, comparisons to other scans, opinions of radiologists and doctors) it was determined that I should have a PET scan. This is a delightful procedure where they shoot radioactive sugar water into your veins and see what lights up. Cancer lights up. But just to complicate matters, other things light up, too. The scan took hours. And yes, the spot lit up but no, the test was not conclusive.

Because of the inconclusiveness of the PET scan my oncologist called to say I should have a biopsy done on my lung. I was driving at the time of the call. I pulled over to the side of the street to talk with her and then cried for about a minute and half. I was so tired. Tired of indetermination; tired of the pokes and pricks. It had been five weeks of the spot niggling at me, thirty-five days of a faint-but-present nagging. It hadn't even been a year since I had finished treatment. Was my life ever going to right itself? Would it ever involve less worry and concern?

After consultation with oncology, interventional radiology, and my integrative team, I decided to have the biopsy. Six weeks after the CT scan that revealed the spot, my lung was biopsied. The following Monday my oncologist called. I was on the road again. But this time Randy was driving and we were on our way home from camping. We were just about to cross the river from Wisconsin into Minnesota.

Dr. Gellar knows how to make a phone call like this. She didn't pause once I picked up the phone but ran her sentences smack up against one another. Thank goodness. "Jeannie, ThisisDrGellarandIhavegoodnews." I didn't even have time to react to the "Jeannie, this is Dr. Gellar" before the "good news" went straight to my brain. In my experience it's rarely good news when one's oncologist is calling. Actually it isn't really good news to even have an oncologist. But this time it was Good News!

So what do I have in that right lung? Apparently it is some kind of pneumonia. There will be another side-trek as they figure out what it is, why it is, and what to do about it. But that is all beside the fact because it's not cancer.

Randy and I went out to dinner after we returned home. We sat outside on a patio on a beautiful autumn night and toasted ourselves. We toasted my lungs and my adorable little spot of pneumonia. I said, in my heart of hearts I did not believe it could be cancer. But, also, my heart of hearts was screaming: *How in the world could this possibly be cancer! The impossibility of it, the ludicrousness!* But, of course, all along I could see the world in which it was cancer, too. I say "of course" because that is the way this new life works. The dualities are often very close together. Click/clack.

Randy and I spent a giddy evening of not-cancer ringing around us. And then the next day we went back to our normal. He went to work, tearing out walls and rebuilding them. I made appointments and did follow-ups, cooked dinner, and tried to keep my thoughts to a minimum. But the rhythmic machine still moves back and forth: *Will my strength and endurance ever return?* Click. *But I did take a two-hour hike.* Clack. *What will the next scan show?* Click. *I should totally buy that sweater.* Clack.

I did get the sweater by the way. So, apparently, I am planning on a future. Does hope and optimism come in a package? Of course not. But I had to laugh yesterday morning when I opened a box from Amazon. In it were six bottles of earth-friendly dish soap. Six bottles! Obviously I got a really great deal but more importantly, sometime in the midst of all the unknowingness about my not-cancer prognosis I made the decision to buy six bottles of dish soap. That just made me smile. I obviously believed all along. It may not be life into my nineties but it is a future—filled with cashmere and dish soap. Luxury and practicality. Click/Clack. I'll take it.

—edited excerpt from CaringBridge ten months after the end of treatment

What the river carries

I am here again (still) beside the river.
Who am I if not this body walking alongside
this other body (of water)

I am watching what little current remains (flowing)
knowing that nothing here is permanent.

The sky has turned purple as I am asking
the river (toward me and away) to take with it
my fallible, tenuous heart; to let me cast

my tears (all salt and memory and loss) into its
shadow where it soothes the (scarred, ancient)
granite by whispering its name.

The river appears frozen but (underneath)
it is alive, pared down to its essential self. At its
edge I am both empty (rendered grief) and full.

The cardinal appears at twilight (fleeting)
the crossroad of this winter's night. I see you
in the quick, red flutter (precious), but also

in the naked branches and the cold, cloudless sky.
The stars begin to glow (joy) as the river and I diverge.

It flows far and away beyond my sight.
I follow the path before me, my heart
thrumming with the cold beauty of the night.

What If This Was Good Enough?

This has been a week of treacherous ice and ridiculous cold. I trekked at my peril (even with my Yaktrax) and Pearl, our rescue pup, had to wear her red jacket—such humiliation. But today is a perfect Minnesota snow day. The bitter cold replaced by freshly fallen snow.

I have been thinking a lot about the New Year, my tabula rasa. Spread out before me like last night's snowfall, 2017 is glistening and unsullied. I can see no defined path. Nothing to say, *go this way.* Even though I know there's a sidewalk underneath all that snow, it's easy to imagine forging my own way. I like all that possibility.

But 2016 isn't finished with me yet. Losing my brother, Larry, last October left me heartbroken and weary. Since then loss and grief, hardly strangers, were again my closest companions. I've struggled with them, but I've learned a lot from them, too. As I wrote my solstice poem, one clear thought came to me. I wasn't seeking the absence of grief. That would be unrealistic. What I was seeking was mutual respect. *I didn't want grief shouting at me.* I didn't want loss to be the only thing on the agenda. I know both will continue to be a part of my inner conversation as they have been since my diagnosis. They still have a lot to tell me. But now I am listening, not arguing, so they don't have to shout to get my attention. Listening is a prerequisite to understanding. I am learning.

I expected to have something mind-blowing to say two years out from treatment. But it's hard to define *any* life in neat, comprehensible paragraphs. Life post–cancer treatment is still messy. It would be easy to say, *Cancer changed my life.* It did. Easy also to say, *I am just so grateful to be alive.*

I am. But how about, *I live every day to my fullest now?* I don't know. It's not that easy.

The year after cancer treatment was a bridge year for me. I was in a state of limbo between chronic illness and a regrouping or almost a homecoming (keeping in mind one can never really go home) to my body. Two years after completion, I am better but still so vulnerable. I've suffered a lot of sickness. The wear and tear on my body from chemo and radiation is showing. My immune system is shot. My muscles are decimated. I have chronic lymphedema in my right leg. I blew out my left knee, tearing both my ACL and my meniscus while dancing. Yes, while dancing.

Cancer takes so much away. There are the obvious casualties—the vitality and the various body parts or organs. But others are less easy to classify or address. The biggest loss is identity, how we once saw ourselves: As that person we once were who seems in retrospect so young, healthy, and maybe a little naïve.

Sometimes I read the obituaries. It may seem morbid, but it is part of my compulsion with disease, death, and my survival so far. When I read, "After a six-year battle with cancer," or "After a ten-year battle with cancer," I know they are counting time from the diagnosis. There may have been years of good life in between. But still there are those cancer brackets around life. When does it become no longer about cancer? Maybe never.

So, sure, the losses keep piling up. The older you get, the more that's going to happen. But I am trying to listen, not argue. I no longer have the time or desire to fight against. I am working *toward*. I may not make Nirvana. Or become a bodhisattva. But I think this right here **is** the holy and the fully. I am trying to live my life with abundance and loss, with grief and gratitude, with mercy, forgiveness, and acceptance. All those biggies. And in that *living life to the fullest* quest, I am allowing that this life right here might just be good enough.

Today at dusk, Randy, Pearl, and I walked alongside the Mississippi River. It was eighteen degrees. Kind of balmy. The moon was full above us. Not a cloud in sight. We made our own path through the freshly fallen snow. The moon followed us, keeping watch. A bright eye in the darkening sky. Before we headed home I turned and looked behind us. Our footprints had completely disappeared. Snow had fallen and drifted inside them, filling their gaps, creating a fresh new plain, one more tabula rasa.

—edited excerpt from CaringBridge two years after the end of treatment

My Life Practice

Someone said to me after my diagnosis that they were curious to see what gifts I might receive on this journey. I was annoyed by that comment at the time. Yet it stayed with me. I resented it initially because I so much resented the cancer. And I resented the idea that somehow these "gifts" would lessen the blow. Or that I might receive these gifts as a payment or reparation for the things I've lost. There was no way to lessen the blow. There was no adequate compensation. Cancer was holding my life hostage. I felt like I paid the ransom but never got my life back.

It's hard to admit but I did find gifts on my cancer journey. They are not recompense. I think of them more like the beauty of a sunset as a wildfire rages and destroys everything in its path. Even though the fire causes ruin and heartbreak it's impossible not to be awestruck by the beauty on the horizon.

All the scars I bear aren't visible. I certainly have memories engraved in flesh—from incisions, my port, and radiation tattoos. But the bigger scars aren't the ones you can see from the outside. So it is with the gifts I received. Some were simple and abundant like the generosity and love from family and friends, even strangers. Writing this book is a blessing because sharing my story makes me feel less alone and allows me to reclaim something of who I was before the intersection with disease.

That I am here at all is the biggest gift, of course; that I have healed to the extent I have: Physically, emotionally, sensually, and spiritually.

I am not the woman I was before cancer. I once hoped I would return to her; that she was just over the next rehabilitative hurdle or around the next healing corner. There was no return to that prior self. But despite my emotional apprehensions, spiritual anxieties, physical debilitation, and missing parts, I am a whole woman. And in some ways, perhaps in the spiritual ways of resiliency, compassion, and gratitude, I am more whole than I ever was. This might have been what my friend meant—the unseen, unrecognized, under-valued gifts of loss.

These gifts are less tangible and more elusive to define. A few days after my diagnosis I wrote in my journal about how I would wake each morning to a gathering storm of panic and dread, that I couldn't sustain those emotions, that I had to build the calm within myself each day. Throughout my struggle with illness and disease I was constantly on a road to acceptance. I chose not to think in battle metaphors. I wasn't waging a war. I never called cancer my enemy. I didn't want my heart filled with anger or to spend the little mental energy I had resisting the idea of what was clearly happening in my body.

Finding peace with my situation meant learning to love what felt broken in my life—my heart, my body, and the cells that went awry. Working toward acceptance didn't mean I was giving up or that I was ready to die. I definitely wanted to live. I wanted to do all I could to eradicate the cancer. But I needed peace to nourish and strengthen this life I was trying so desperately to save. The wheels of anger would have only spun me deeper into a rut of misery and left me bitter, grasping after a way of life that was no longer attainable. The problem with grasping I discovered is that it's insatiable. It's a hunger nothing can satisfy. More importantly, if I were angry, if I was always reaching, always looking at what I didn't have, I wouldn't see the beauty that was there in front of me.

I was, and still am, a novice in the art of acceptance. It is a practice like any other—yoga, meditation, poetry, or prayer. Any success I have had feels like a gift—like I am strengthening a muscle—a muscle that I will need in a life that will continue to be uncertain.

Each year away from my diagnosis anniversary or from the end of my treatment with no recurrence means something significant in terms of my prognosis. The chances of my survival grow stronger. But I am always aware of my disease and my odds. I am aware, also, that when I hear someone has died after six years with cancer, that they may have lived with remission for two of those years, that for a while they may have felt like they beat the odds.

I resonate to the title of Maya Angelou's book, *Wouldn't Take Nothing for My Journey Now*. The most important word for me in the title is **now**. I wouldn't take nothing **now**. Initially, after my diagnosis, I would have taken anything to have this journey erased from my future. At so many points along the path I would have welcomed an easier route. If I could have, I would have detoured this whole cancer road wreck.

But there was no detour. There was only what was before me. Since I couldn't go around it, I went through it. Right now, I am here and grateful.

(poem)

still
of water,
flowing
toward me and away
all salt and memory and loss
scarred, ancient
underneath
rendered grief,
fleeting,
precious
joy

Buoyancy, the Movie

> *"If you ask me what I came into this life to do, I will tell you: I came to live out loud."*
> *— Emile Zola*

Shortly after my surgery, my dear friend and fellow video producer, Will Hommeyer, came to visit. He brought an ebullient bouquet of purple and white lilacs, their branches bent with the weight of full, heady blooms. Lilacs are my favorite—the perfect ephemeral embodiment of Minnesota spring. They infused the space with sweet splendor.

After gentle hugs and surgical small talk we took a walk with Sadie, the dog. It was a slow, pensive stroll in what would have been a flawless spring day if I hadn't just been diagnosed with cancer, if I hadn't just had a hysterectomy. The creek beside us was full from spring rains, frantically racing to join with the mighty Mississippi. Trees were shimmering in electric green leafiness. Bushes sparked with small white buds. All of nature seemed overtly alive, vibrating with fecundity.

Somewhere along our meandering I lost track of our conversation. My brain was fuzzy. In those early days I was constantly engaged in an internal soliloquy, running the numbers on how old my children and grandchildren would be at the time of my death if I survived the year, or three years, or seven. I quieted the fretful chatter and returned to our conversation. Will was mentioning a dream he had and an idea of a project we could work on together. I realized he had proposed we make a documentary about my journey through cancer treatment. I was overwhelmed, my body was sore and sutured together; my spirit was flailing around for something that would tether it. But I remember thinking, yes. I wouldn't agree until I talked to Randy and our children but as I turned the idea over in my head I could envision this movie. I saw myself before the camera searching for meaning, for the right words and imagery. I saw how the movie might provide another portal through which I could glimpse a glimmer of the mystery.

Although it was still only May, and I had many long months of treatment before me, I knew a deep wound would be exposed for all to see if I chose to document my cancer journey. It was a wound that was secretive and scary. A gynecological cancer is a private cancer. It felt like a huge risk but worthwhile in order to intimately and artfully explore what was going on in my body and spirit. As a poet I wrote openly about my life. I hoped that the documentary would be a natural extension of that willingness.

When I initially talked to Randy about the possibility of the documentary he asked me, *"Isn't this surreal enough for you?"* Of course, it was. It was surreal enough. My known world was falling apart. So many people were coming to my aid—doctors, family, and friends to support, love, and try to heal me. But in my poetry and in the documentary, I felt I was answering a call. Creating art out of my heartbreak felt like giving my soul a mission. Instead of making it more surreal I hoped the documentary would create sense out of chaos, ground me in the moment, and give my spirit something on which to tether itself.

I don't remember the next conversation with Will, the one in which I must have said, "Yes, let's do this." But we commenced. Although I felt privileged to be the subject of this film, it was very challenging. My energy was nil and what little I had I tried to save for healing. But as the film progressed I had to get permission to shoot in radiation, chemo, acupuncture clinics, salons, and doctor offices. I requested and scheduled interviews with doctors and family members. I helped Will craft the interview questions. I also tried to be articulate as chemo, emotions, and sheer exhaustion robbed me of my memory and comprehension. Sometimes in the middle of an answer I would just start crying. Or as I say in the film, my brain would go sideways. Will was patient and just kept rolling until eventually I came up with some kind of answer. I imagine he got more than he bargained for when interviews with me stretched for hours.

As people learned about the project they were often surprised, even dumbfounded that I would share such a personal story. Some say that I was brave. I don't feel brave, at least not about the filming. It was a profound honor to be in the seat opposite of Will and his lens. This movie would never have been made with any other filmmaker. Will and I have known each other for over thirty years. We have worked together, supported one another, eaten meals together, shared our joys and miseries. I knew him to be a careful craftsman, an artist with integrity. Most importantly, I trusted him with my story.

Recently I was part of a healing group. We all sat in a circle with our various afflictions and vexations. At the opening of each session the facilitator would ask us to share our *cheers and challenges.* Every week I was surprised that they were one and the same for me. My greatest joys were also my biggest challenges. But isn't that often the way with our dearest things? Right up to and including our closest relationships. Balance is just shifting perspective. Close one eye and all my joys line up before me. Close the other eye and there are only challenges. Both eyes give me the whole picture.

One of my favorite aspects of the healing group was the opportunity for real emotional intimacy with people I had only just met. Shared trauma has a way of breaking down superficial barriers between people. Illness creates alienation. Sick people feel they live outside of normal life. We experience a sense of otherness but sharing our vulnerability and exposing our soft bellies to one another reduces, if not eliminates, the sense of alienation.

Throughout my illness when I have been at my lowest, when I felt the sting of otherness and the exhaustion of trying to keep afloat, it was often the act of sharing my vulnerability that buoyed me up and helped rebuild my calm. Laying bare my pain, exposing the gaping abyss at my feet, acknowledging the internal soliloquy with my community through conversation, my writing and particularly within the context of producing *Buoyancy*, both the film and this book, helped me find the ballast at my core.

When I reflect on that prescient walk in May, it is this intimacy and connection magnified and duplicated by the camera's lens that elicited that intuitive yes. On the surface

I may have thought I could catch a glimpse into the mystery of illness or find an answer to the incessant questions of *Why me?* But there was something larger at work. Something greater than my own pain and suffering. The movie was an intimate dialogue with an audience that was both beside me and beyond me. It brought me from the solitary confinement of illness into the freedom of living out loud.

Praise

> *"Praise, my dear one/Let us disappear into praising/*
> *Nothing belongs to us"—Rainer Maria Rilke*

Does not even this body
belong to me? Or I to it?
My imperfect machine,
no warranty and all this work
it's done for me. The humiliation
we suffered in that dismal
darkness when first it stumbled,
then faltered, and fell from
homeostasis.

And what of spirit? The
wildness that has hurled me
into and out of love until
I thought I could take no more.
No more nakedness, no more
grief. Yet, stripped bare,
with luminous forgiveness,
I took more.

Of course, tomorrow
never belonged to me.
Although, I pestered it
with questions. How far will
this path take me? Where is
the limit of my longing? Will
I ever relinquish desire?

What is most mine
is faith in absence;
The losses I carry with me,
tucked into my pocket,
not hidden in pity, but resting
beside me, a gentle shimmer,
the hopefulness in this great
Unknowing, and in the hollow
left by what has disappeared.
This is what belongs to me.

All this I praise.

Afterward

When she called, I answered my phone with great enthusiasm. "Hey, Jeannie! How are you?" There was a brief silence. Jeannie is not known for her silence, brief or otherwise. She responded slowly, saying that she had something to tell me. My heart dropped to the floor as she explained her devastating diagnosis.

We had been scheduled to launch a new project together as soon as she returned home from Belize. Now, instead, she was going into surgery for a complete hysterectomy, followed by months of chemotherapy and radiation.

My immediate impulse was to document her journey. I wanted to use my camera to tap her words and witness her passage as she stumbled down the rabbit hole of cancer treatment with all the uncertainty it entailed. I tried to talk myself out of it. Maybe it was a crazy idea; I needed to be there for her as a friend, not as a filmmaker. But the idea kept circling back around and I could not shake it from my thoughts.

Jeannie and I have been good friends for over thirty years and counting. Throughout much of that time, we have been colleagues working together in the film industry. She is the godmother of my eldest daughter, Camille. We were like family and I felt a responsibility to act, to do something to capture and preserve the essence of this amazing woman for her kids, her grandchildren, her husband, and for me; to hold on to a dear friend who could otherwise slip from my grasp.

Just nights before Jeannie's call, I had a dream about the two of us working together on an independent film project. It was something esoteric and complicated that involved poetry. When I woke up, I could not recall what the film had been about.

A few days after her surgery, Jeannie and I took an unhurried walk together along Minnehaha Creek. I told her about my dream and asked, "What would you say to the idea of letting me document your journey?" She was immediately open to the idea, provided Randy agreed. He did, albeit reluctantly. We commenced filming immediately. This was not the film made from dreams, but in an odd, mystical twist, we were working together on a new movie.

My previous documentary work had always been well planned and researched. This was a new way of working; spontaneous and immediate. I had to use my intuition and trust my relationship with Jeannie to access the story. I often didn't know if I had permission to film in the clinic until I arrived at the door with my camera in hand. There were no second takes. It all unfurled in real time. I had to be completely open to the way the story evolved.

As it turned out, I was given broad access behind the scenes. It was an odd feeling to find myself in spaces in the hospital where even Jeannie's husband was not permitted to go. I wrestled with the need to be in the midst of the action, but at the same time not be invasive. This was a tension that I was only able to navigate because of my friendship with Jeannie. I did not need to worry about being overly polite. I knew that Jeannie understood the process of making a film and would push back if I was unwelcome.

From the first, the act of making the film together was a vital forum for Jeannie to process her story. What surprised me was the resilient narrative form that emerged from the chaos that cancer brings to one's life and how I vicariously came face-to-face with my own mortality. Jeannie chose to live in beauty and buoyancy rather than in fear and anxiety. For that, I am in awe. Her tenacity and spirit profoundly impacted the way I lean into my life with renewed intention and gratitude. It was a deeply intimate experience to walk beside her on this bold adventure. I am eternally grateful for all that she has taught me about living in dualities.

—*Will Hommeyer, filmmaker, photographer*

Acknowledgments

I don't believe there is a formula for surviving cancer. Regardless of countless articles and books I read about chaga mushrooms, colonics, immunotherapy, anti-inflammatory diet, and positive affirmations, it seems that survival often comes down to a roll of the dice. Our genes, family and community, the environment in which we live or work, the severity of the diagnosis, all contribute to our potential recovery or failure. There are factors that influence the outcome such as diet, exercise, age, income, and access to good healthcare. But a lot of mystery and conjecture surround disease and resiliency.

Although I had an unfortunate diagnosis, I was lucky in so many ways. I am overwhelmed with gratitude and awe for the love and gifts of generosity I received. It's difficult to adequately acknowledge all the love and support I had to get to this point in my story. If in the words below I have forgotten anyone, I apologize in advance. Please know that even the smallest kindness mattered greatly to me

Much love and appreciation always and forever to my husband—Randy, the stalwart, my pillar. Thank you for staying married to me, and for continually evolving with me to accommodate our shifting landscape. We are still here together. Profound love and appreciation to my children, Nathan, Chelsea, and Luke, who over and over again came to my aid with their love, food, walks, accompanying me to doctor appointments, MRI, chemo, and so much more. And to my grandchildren for always giving me reason to smile and hope. Sadie, the wonder dog, for being beside me throughout the journey and to Pearl who is nascent and has big paw prints to fill but just might be up for the challenge.

Chelsea and her husband, Ian, were our medical interpreters and go-to experts. Chelsea took on the responsibility of nurse but never forgot her role of daughter so she cried on the couch with me but also oversaw many aspects of medical care. A special thanks to my son-in-law, Dr. Ian Schwartz, who wore the Superman cape during my cancer protocol. After diagnosis he researched and found the best doctor, took time off work to come to appointments, literally walked beside me as they took me to surgery and, unbelievably, was the first face I saw coming out of recovery, saying my name, letting me know I was safe. He helped keep the calm when all was confusion and disorder. I am eternally grateful.

Much gratitude to my siblings and their families. I am very thankful to my sister Nancy for her support in the tangibles of wigs, pins, scarves, and recipes but also for the wise counsel. She gave me new perspectives to consider when I was at my lowest. Thank you to Lance, Larry, and Marcy, and Jerry and Dail for all the support. Thank you to Kris for the love and yoga nidra! Thank you to all my nieces and nephews.

Thank you to Bev and Michael for propping us up in all our leaning places; for the visits, cooking, counsel, and care. To all my in-law Anderson family—you are my example for unconditional love. Thank you for the support and encouragement whether in person, by package, or email.

Thank you to my extended family—Michael Bassett, always and forever, one of my truest friends. Thank you for dropping everything to come stay with us to help twice during the course of treatment and for giving so much love in word and deed. Will Hommeyer for constant witnessing, for listening to me for hours on end, and for friendship through it all. Thank you to J. Otis Powell‽, a constant source of poetry and commiseration. Thank you for praying to me. I miss you. To Flo for everything from food to flowers, words to wisdom. Dear Cilla for being the first person outside my family to hear the news and holding me in her love. The Sistren for ritual and love. To Janis for so much support including: Delivering uplifting movies, headbands, and scarves, lunches, love, and laughter. Amy, for filling my empty bowls metaphorically and nutritionally, for the brilliant idea of my girl party and for hosting it! Ruth for co-hosting the party with verve and style. Thank you to all the beautiful women who came together to encourage me by bringing poetry, food, seashells, rocks, and wonder. Thank you to Blue Moon for the care and accommodation, for being the best crew. And to Janice Porter who is always in my heart, inspiring me.

Much gratitude to my medical team who were all so proficient, generous, and compassionate: Dr. Gellar, Dr. Dusenbury, Cara Miller, APRN CNP, Dr Bucher. Acupuncturists Bobbee Vang and Jessica Hanson, Shiatsu therapist Sally Schroeder, and all the amazing nurses, assistants, and radiation techs. Thank you to the institutions: Masonic Cancer Clinic, U of MN Hospital, Penny George, and Pathways A Healing Center. Thank you President Obama for the ACA which allowed us some dignity in paying our health premiums and medical expenses.

Thank you to Mark Myers for creating the Motherland benefit and including me. To everyone who contributed to its success—Scott Herald with Rock the Cause and Andrea Swensson of The Current; the bands: Apollo Cobra, Joey Verskotzi, and Astrobeard; the businesses that donated to the silent auction: Sovereign Grounds, Chinook Book, Bryn Mawr Soap, Bikes and Pieces, Do It Green, Moss Envy, Pumphouse Creamery, Classic Tae Kwon Do Studio, Bernie King and the Guilty Pleasures, and Douglas Ewert, plus many more.

Thank you again to Will Hommeyer for organizing my 60th birthday and fundraiser for *Buoyancy* the film. Thank you to all the good people who attended, danced, toasted, and levitated me. Much gratitude to the Brass Messengers and to, Bernie King and the Guilty Pleasures who provided the tunes.

For the writing of this book many people corresponded with me through CaringBridge and Facebook, read my posts and poems, and encouraged me to write this book. To Will (again) who created the movie which inspired the book and contributed his beautiful photographs. To all my readers who read many edits of this book: Always my first reader, Randy, also A. P. Porter, Nancy Brandt, Flo Golod (who read above and beyond the call of friendship!), Shari Albers, and Amy Ballestad. Thank you to the fabulous Dara

Syrkin, my first editor, who has my undying gratitude for so much insight into the heart of this memoir. And to Sue Filbin, editor, artist and book designer, who envisioned the book from the very beginning, who acted as midwife, consultant, and friend; who was always accommodating, patient, and clever.

Thank you, Minnesota, for all your green spaces; for the many spots of nature that provide me with healing and contemplation including Minnehaha Creek and Parkway, Mississippi River, and all the Minnesota state parks. Thank you to countless authors and poets who provided me with insight, inspiration, and beauty.

To all those who cooked for me, gave me rides, brought me hats and scarves, walked with me, massaged my feet, cleaned my house, found resources, fundraised, sent flowers, poems, cards and endless encouragement, partied with me, supported the movie. For all my chemo-sabes, and my chemo-poets, for the brave ones who talked honestly and for ones who hardly knew what to say but whose hearts were breaking, I am ever grateful for the love manifested in action.

Gayle Adelsman
Shari Albers
Louis Alemayehu
Bobbie Anderson
Candy Anderson
Clayton and Liz Anderson
Jan and Arthur Anderson
Lucinda Anderson
Michael Anderson

Cathy and Charlie Anhut
Rondi Atkin
Amy Ballestad
Scott Bartell
Michael Bassett
Titilayo Bediako
Kris Bishop
Mary Bohman
Carolyn & Kirt Boston
Nancy Brandt
Liam Brennan
Olivia Carideo
Melinda Carter
Kim Christiansen
Bill Cottman
Sharon Davis
John Dehn
Camille Einstein
Robin Epstein
Susie Erickson
Janis Lane Ewert
Kurt and Rosie Faber
Joe Fieber
Sue and Dan Filbin
Cheri Galbraith
Lindsey Galbraith
Adel Gardner
Frieda Gardner
Fikret and Fahira Gerzic
Paul Gitz
Flo Golod

Joann and Ewen Ha
Mike Hazard
Maren Hinderlie
Will Hommeyer
Kinshasha Kambui
Lisa Karina
Jane Leach
Bayla MacDougal
Jenny MacDougal
Mark Maida
Sue Ann Martinson
Margo McCreary
Mark & Lindsey Myers
Meredith Myers
Susie Oppenheim
Warren and Patty Park
Ruth Patton
Ben Petro
Anthony P Porter
J Otis Powell‽
Lynette Reini-Grandall
Mike Rollin
Lily Rothbart
Paul Rucker
Steve Sandberg
Penny Schafer
Linda Schreiber
Wolfie Schwartz
Geri Segal
Thomas Smith
Beverly Sonen

Sandy Spieler
Lotus Stack
Sylvia Storvick
Rick and Kay Streng
Tracey Stretch
Tressa Sularz
Jeff Sylvertre
Jeannie Tazzioli
Jill van Koolwijk
Vizi Salon
Cilla Walford
Morgan Grayce Willow
Josie Wilson

About the Author

Photo by Will Hommeyer

Jeannie Piekos is an award-winning poet, arts activist, and art grandma. She is the author of the chapbook, *Held Up To The Light*. She feels lucky to live in Minneapolis—surrounded by green space, creeks, rivers, and a bunch of lakes—with her husband Randy and dog Pearl. She lives very near to her three children and five grandchildren. When she travels far from this loving base she returns home with fresh eyes and a grateful heart.